SCHOOL DIDN'T TEACH YOU THIS

The Real Rules Of Money

School Didn't Teach You This

Published by:
Sticky Novels LLC
201 York Road, Suite 1-522
Jenkintown, PA 19046
Copyright@StickyNovels.com
Visit: www.TheColorsOfMoney.com

ISBNs:
E-book Edition: 979-8-9999140-1-9
Paperback Edition: 979-8-9999140-2-6
Library of Congress Control Number: 2026905314
BISAC Subject Headings:
BUS050000 — Business & Economics / Personal Finance / General
BUS027000 — Business & Economics / Finance / Financial Planning
SEL031000 — Self-Help / Personal Growth / Success

Disclaimer:

This book is intended for educational and informational purposes only. The strategies, opinions, and systems presented herein reflect the personal experiences and research of the author and are not intended as financial, legal, tax, or investment advice.

Readers are advised to consult licensed professionals—including certified financial planners, tax advisors, and attorneys—before making any financial decisions based on the content of this book. Every individual's circumstances are unique, and what worked for others may not be suitable or effective for you.

The author and publisher make no guarantees regarding financial outcomes, income generation, or investment returns. Past results of any referenced individuals or case studies do not promise or imply future success for any reader.

Trademark Notice:

The Colors of Money Press™ is a trademark of Sticky Novels LLC.

The Colors of Money™ is a proprietary financial framework developed by Robyn La'More. It is a common law trademark of Robyn La'More and is currently pending registration with the United States Patent and Trademark Office. Unauthorized use or reproduction of the system, names, or symbols is strictly prohibited without written permission.

Credits:
Author: Ms. Robyn La'More
Book Cover Concept: Robyn La'More

Printed in the United States of America
First Edition: April 2025
10 9 8 7 6 5 4 3 2 1

SCHOOL DIDN'T TEACH YOU THIS

The Real Rules Of Money

ROBYN LA'MORE

COLORS OF MONEY
PRESS

This book is dedicated to my father,
Joe Young (1934–2025)

You were the first Black man I ever saw be self-employed.
Being a private contractor in a world of employees was a powerful
environmental influence—more than I realized at the time.
I, too, became self-employed—even when I thought I was a businesswoman.
Now I understand the distinction.
When my passions lead, I may become self-employed with certain entities.
With others, I will be a businesswoman—and at other times, an investor.
It all began with you, Daddy.
A leader, a strong man, a powerful example.
I thank you for giving me more than you had to spare—
For reaching for heights you didn't even know how to achieve.
I'll take it from here.
I love you—I miss you, Daddy.
And parts of me will miss you well into my next lifetime.

ACKNOWLEDGMENTS

Thank you to my editor, Lisa Day, and to the beta readers who helped shape this book with their honest feedback.

To my formatter, Brady, thank you for the exceptional work you've done on my fiction and for breaking your own rules to join me in the nonfiction space. Your courage, kindness, and technical precision are inspiring. I'm deeply grateful for your willingness to grow with me and apply your talent across genres.

To Colors of Money Press, thank you for your belief in this work and your support throughout the publishing process.

To the mentors who shaped how I see ownership, wealth, and financial structure:

John Kluge Sr. was the first person I ever witnessed build an empire rooted in residual income. He understood media before the world caught up, acquiring syndication rights and full control of broadcast networks while others were still leasing airtime or licensing shows without owning the underlying content. That moment planted the seed.

To Diana Ross, for more reasons than I could ever list. But when she took over her own career and created Anaid Productions, it was the first time I realized a Black woman could own her own corporation. She's the reason I dared to form my first company—as a teenager. Like her, I used my name spelled backwards. A powerful act of self-empowerment. Thank you, Ms. Ross.

Later, Oprah Winfrey would create Harpo Inc., along with all of its eventual subsidiaries, also her name spelled backward. She provided both love and leadership for a generation. I was there watching from the very first show, had the extraordinary pleasure of later visiting Harpo Studios, and missed only a handful of episodes during her twenty-five-year run.

Her example of media ownership continues to inspire me. Thank you, Ms. Winfrey.

And now, Tyler Perry stands as my living blueprint for what it means to merge the highest levels of business and creativity in the media space. Thank you, Mr. Perry.

To my renowned stylist and dear friend Ellin Lavar—thank you for keeping my big hair beautiful, and my thoughts grounded. You've been more than a stylist, you've been an accessible, successful businesswoman I could ask real questions and learn from without ego or distance.

To the Center City branch of the Free Library of Philadelphia, thank you. Before there was internet access in every home, I studied money, economics, and business theory through your biographies and back issues. You were my first financial education center.

I've had many teachers, but two changed my life: Carlstene L. Pryer and Ms. Dolores Petty (R.I.P.). Your guidance during my most difficult years became part of the foundation I stand on now.

To my family: In loving memory of my father—your presence is profoundly missed, but your influence is forever. To my mother, who could stretch a dollar further than anyone thought possible, I love you. To my brother Rome, thank you for your steady presence and unwavering support. You remain a source of strength in an unstable world.

I extend my deepest appreciation, gratitude, acknowledgment, and love to Aunt Sis, Big Brother Gino, Juliet, Janita, Special K (Karen), and of course, Dallas—I love you all.

To my past and present staff across various ventures, thank you for working with a then-teenage boss still learning the ropes. With my teenage years now in the distance, I continue to learn as much from great staff as I hope you've learned from me.

To the readers, you inspired me to write what I had only lived in fits and starts, rarely with any continuity. Daddy was right again: *"Baby, what you need is a high level of consistency."*

This book is my effort toward that goal—teaching and being accountable. The adult work of growing up, not just aging.

To each of you on your own journey, know that you gave me the courage to publish this, my first nonfiction book, and the purpose to build what I hope becomes a financial movement, one rooted in truth, ownership, and strategy.

Thank you for believing in me, through your investment of both time and money. It is my deepest intention that you receive a handsome return on both.

- Robyn La'More

"Building residual income through syndication and licensing gave me wealth long after the initial deal."

— JOHN W. KLUGE SR.

"Only by owning who and what you are can you step into the fullness of life."

— OPRAH WINFREY, *WHAT I KNOW FOR SURE* (2014)

"After over twenty years with the label, I returned to Motown as a part-owner."

— DIANA ROSS

"Ownership changes everything... I own the lights. I own the sets. Because I own everything, my returns are higher."

— TYLER PERRY

"While everybody was fighting for a seat at the table... I said, 'Y'all... I'll be down in Atlanta building my own.' Own your stuff. Own your business. Own your way."

— TYLER PERRY, BET AWARDS SPEECH

"The best investment you can make is in yourself. The more you learn, the more you earn."

— WARREN BUFFETT

CONTENTS

INTRODUCTION

Some of what we're taught about money is dead wrong—most of it is just incomplete.

We're taught how to earn money. We're taught how to spend it. We're even taught to save a little, if we're lucky. But we're rarely taught how money actually works—how it moves, multiplies, and escapes.

The education system is the worst at preparing you for financial freedom.

This book isn't about budgeting. It's not about pinching pennies or depriving yourself of joy.

It's about a paradigm shift: everything you spend is not real money, and every dollar you earn is not equal in purpose or power to make you wealthy.

This book will give you the clarity, tools, and habits that lead to ownership, power, and freedom. It's about breaking the cycle of paycheck dependence and building something that lasts.

You won't find fluff here.

I wrote this for people who are ready to shift—people who want more, but don't want to wait on luck, lottery tickets, or some mythical raise to get it. You'll find real strategies, plain language, and powerful concepts that are often hidden behind industry jargon or reserved for people born into wealth.

Some of what's inside might challenge you. It might piss you off. That's okay. That means it's working. Growth always stings at first. But once you see the matrix, you can't unsee it. And once you start taking control—even one small step at a time—you begin to reclaim your time, your energy, and your financial future.

This book is short, sharp, and actionable by design.

As a novelist, I could've written something three times the length. But I fought every instinct to compete with other financial books on word count or page number. My decision? To give you only the best—distilled to what you can read in one sitting and begin implementing immediately.

Each chapter stands on its own but builds momentum. You don't need an economics degree. Just a willingness to see money differently, dynamically.

I'll introduce you to a paradigm-shifting concept I call The Colors of Money™. I believe in this idea so strongly, I'm devoting my second book to it. But for now, this one will give you what you need to:

– understand your relationship with money,

– identify which income stream (which **color**) you're relying on,

– and recognize the ones you haven't yet accessed.

You'll learn why small capital gains are a cheat code to acquiring assets —and how those assets can eventually become passive income.

You'll also learn what passive income really is... and what it's not.

There's a lot you weren't taught.

But it's not too late.

You're here now.

Your march toward green money starts today—with one change, one flip, one investment in you.

Prepare to learn what school never taught you.

Let's begin.

ONE
MONEY IS A MIRROR

Behavior First. Budget Later.

💡 CONCEPT:

Your relationship with money isn't just about dollars—it's a reflection of how you see yourself, your choices, and your beliefs. Money doesn't lie; it simply reflects. Your values, financial knowledge, and future trajectory are revealed in every transaction with money.[1]

———

🧠 THEORY

Financial behaviors mirror internal patterns: scarcity, fear, entitlement, confidence, worthiness. If you want to change how money shows up in your life, you have to examine how you show up around money. Psychology—not just budgeting—drives your outcome.[2]
   Scarcity mindset vs abundance behavior
   Emotional spending as self-soothing
   Avoidance of money = avoidance of truth

Believing money is evil vs believing money is everything—both distort your relationship with it[3]

———

❌ MYTH VS. ✅ REALITY

❌ **Myth** "If I just made more money, I'd be fine."

Truth/ Reality: More money magnifies your existing patterns. Overspenders overspend more. Avoiders avoid harder. Fear doesn't disappear with a comma and more zeros.[4]

It's not the amount. Money habits don't change with more zeros—just the magnitude.

Reality

✅ People sabotage raises because they don't feel worthy[5]
✅ Sudden windfalls disappear without new behaviors[6]
✅ Financial denial or avoidance causes slow decay
✅ Your financial reality is a direct translation of your money beliefs—conscious or not[7]

———

📊 ACTION PLAN

- **Self-audit:** What emotion comes up most often when you think about money? Guilt? Fear? Shame? Power? Identify it.
- **Behavior reflection:** Track how you act when money enters or exits your life. Do you over-celebrate, hide, spend impulsively, shut down?
- **Money comfort:** Are you comfortable holding money—or does it burn a hole in your psyche? Track how long you keep money in your possession before you mentally spend it. Not budgeted—spent. Was it impulsive, anxious, avoidant?

- **Write it out:** Journal your money story. Start with: "Growing up, money meant..."
- **Catch the mirror:** For 7 days, notice when you make money-related decisions. Pause. Ask: What does this reflect about me?
- **Set an identity anchor:** Choose a belief that empowers. Example: "I am someone who handles money with clarity and confidence."[8]

———

🧭 WHY THIS MATTERS (AND WHERE IT FITS INTO THE BIGGER PLAN)

This chapter sets the foundation for the entire book. If money reflects who you are—not just what you have—then every future change starts from within. Before we build new systems, set goals, or talk about assets, we need to meet the person who's been making the money decisions all along: you. The mirror doesn't lie, but it can transform—when you do.

———

💥 READY FOR MORE?

If money is a mirror, then the reflection it shows you is a relationship—one that's either growing or breaking down. But most people never treat it like that. They ghost it, avoid it, or let it become toxic. Before we change the numbers, we need to confront the relationship behind them. Let's examine this in the next chapter.

———

📌 FOOTNOTES & CITATIONS:

Sources and citations for this chapter can be found in the back of the book under "Footnotes and Citations."

TWO

DEVELOP YOUR
RELATIONSHIP WITH MONEY

Why it's time to stop ghosting your finances.

💡 CONCEPT:

Money isn't just a number. It's a relationship—dynamic, emotional, sometimes toxic, but always telling. And just like any relationship, it reflects who you are and how you treat it. If you ignore it, it fades. If you obsess over it, it might run. But if you respect it, nurture it, and understand it—it will grow.[1]

This chapter reframes the way we interact with money. Not as a cold tool or distant reward, but as something alive in your life: a conversation partner, a reflection, a partner in your decisions.

———

🧠 THEORY:

Money, though inanimate, moves like energy. It multiplies under structure, disappears under fear, and mirrors our beliefs back to us.[2] So many people are locked in toxic cycles—sabotaging money to prove worth, rejecting it before it rejects them, or burning through it the moment it appears.[3] Especially for those raised on survival economics or public assistance, the relationship with money often feels like a test of loyalty or morality: if you have too much, you'll lose help. If you save, you're punished. If you spend, at least you're "honest."[4]

This trauma doesn't disappear when your income rises. It just shape-shifts. You might earn more, but still feel unsafe. You might accumulate some, but still be afraid to look. You might dream of more, but silently believe you're not supposed to keep it.

That's not discipline. That's an invisible script running your financial life. And it needs to be rewritten.[5]

❌ MYTH VS. ✅ REALITY

❌ *Myth:* Money is a fixed thing. You either have it or you don't.

✅ *Reality:* Money is fluid. It's also emotional. It wants direction, and if you don't give it any, it will find chaos.[6]

The relationship you have with money isn't just measured by your bank balance. It's measured by your behavior, your beliefs, and your visibility into what's really going on. Avoidance is a relationship choice. So is panic spending. So is hiding.

If you've ever tossed bills in a drawer, or let unopened emails pile up in your inbox because you "already know" you can't pay them—this chapter is calling you in, not calling you out. That's a symptom of relationship strain. But all relationships can heal.

You don't need to be rich to feel powerful. You need to be present.[7]

📊 ACTION PLAN

1. 👉 ***Find out where you are.***

No games. Open your accounts. Look at your bills. Count your cash. Add up what you owe. How much red money (debt or damage control) is in play? How much yellow money (passive income)? Green money (second generation passive income)? Orange money (passive potential)? White money (unbudgeted savings)?

You need to know. Why? Because relationships can't evolve if you don't even know where you stand.

2. 👉 *Stop ghosting your bills.*

Don't stuff them in a drawer or let them pile up unread in your email. Yes, it hurts to look when you feel like you can't fix it—but clarity is the first act of courage. Decide when you will sit down each week and do a 15-minute money check-in. Make it sacred. Light a candle if you need to. This is you tending your relationship.

3. 👉 *Touch your money.*

Friction is good. Don't live 100% digitally if you're still emotionally distant from money. Touch some cash. Look at your change. Track what category it came from—this is where The Colors of Money™ come in. Money becomes more real when you feel its weight. Especially when you spend it.[8]

4. 👉 *Respect the purpose of your money.*

Not all dollars are the same. There's a difference between spending orange money on a long-term asset vs. spending red money impulsively just to feel better. Each dollar you touch has a role. Honor that.

5. 👉 *Start using constraints as care.*

A category limit isn't punishment. It's structure. That's what builds trust. If you always overspend in one area, create a visible cap. Know that the boundary is there not to restrict you, but to protect your long-term intimacy with your goals.

—

🧭 WHY THIS MATTERS (AND WHERE IT FITS INTO THE BIGGER PLAN)

You can't plant seeds if you're too scared to look at the dirt. And you can't grow fruit if you've built your identity around staying broke just to qualify for help.

Whether you were raised on survival checks, scarcity narratives, or even generational wealth you weren't taught how to manage—your relationship with money was shaped by someone else's rules.

But now, you're building your own.

The point of this chapter isn't to shame your past. It's to create space for a new future. One where your relationship with money is calm. Focused. Collaborative. You're no longer chasing or avoiding it—you're planning with it.

Every healthy relationship needs visibility, voice, and vision. That's what your money needs, too.

Check in. Set boundaries. Make decisions together. And yes, even forgive yourself for where you've been.

This is how money stops being a monster in the closet and starts becoming a partner in your legacy.

It's time to stop ghosting your finances—and start texting them back.

—

💥 READY FOR MORE?

A better relationship with money doesn't mean fantasizing about having more of it. That's where most people get stuck. They think more zeroes will fix the mess—more income, bigger checks, fatter tax returns. But zeros don't heal bad habits. They expose them.[9]

Before you chase more, fix the foundation. Otherwise, you'll just upgrade the chaos. Let's examine this in the next chapter.

—

📌 FOOTNOTES & CITATIONS:

Sources and citations for this chapter can be found in the back of the book under "Footnotes and Citations.""

THREE
HABITS BEAT ZEROES

Fix the Foundation Before You Add More Floors

💡 CONCEPT:

A million dollars won't fix your money habits. It magnifies them.[1]

Zeroes don't heal broken structures. They expose them.

Imagine thinking it's easier to build a 150-story skyscraper than it is to fix your crumbling two-story house.

That's how most people treat money.

They dream of expansion while ignoring the cracks in their basement.

In this chapter, we're tearing that fantasy down and rebuilding—one habit at a time.

————

🧠 THEORY:

Money doesn't solve behavior. It amplifies it.[2]

Give an impulsive spender $500K—they'll end up in deeper debt, just with better shoes.

Give a builder $5K—they'll multiply it, lose some, learn, and try again.

The math isn't magic. The muscle is in the habits.

Every "zero" you add to your bank account just turns up the volume on your discipline—or your dysfunction.[3] If you haven't fixed the leaks in your financial plumbing, more pressure will just blow the whole system out.

Want passive income? Cool. But you don't earn a dividend from chaos.

You earn it from systems. And systems come from habits.[4]

Habits are boring until they're brilliant.

They don't look sexy until the scoreboard does.

And most people never get there. Why?

Because they're busy fantasizing about skyscrapers instead of learning how to pour concrete.

———

❌ MYTH VS. ✅ REALITY

❌ **Myth:** "If I just made more money, I'd be fine."

✅ **Reality:** If you made more money, your problems would just wear nicer shoes.[5]

The truth hurts because it's clean.

You don't need a windfall—you need a Wednesday routine.

You don't need a lottery ticket—you need a lunch plan that doesn't drain your account.

You don't need a raise—you need a reason to stop outsourcing your decisions to emotion.

Think about this:

If someone gave you a million dollars today,

would your life get better or just faster and louder in the wrong direction?[6]

It's not judgment. It's math and muscle memory.

A million dollars dropped on a shaky structure leads to collapse.

But stack a hundred dollars a week on a stable foundation?

That's how you build upward—quietly, consistently, and permanently.

———

📊 ACTION PLAN

Here's how to turn habits into your superpower and stop worshipping the lottery fantasy.

Step 1: 👉 **Audit the building.**

Ask yourself:

- What are the "weak beams" in your current money life?
- Where are you bleeding cash, leaking time, or stalling progress?
- Be honest. No shame—just blueprint review.

Step 2: 👉 **Fix the foundation before adding floors.**

That means:

- Plug the leaks.
- Track your spending.
- Clean up your language around money ("I'm bad at this" → "I'm learning this").
- If your current two-story house can't handle stress, you're not ready for level three.

Step 3: 👉 **Stack your systems.**

One habit at a time. Not five. Not all at once.
Start with:

- Weekly money check-ins (15 mins)
- Daily spending awareness (track 3 purchases/day)
- Biweekly review of debt and savings targets
- Automate where you can, but don't hide behind automation. Systems need eyeballs until they're muscle memory.[7]

Step 4: 👉 Ignore the applause. Focus on the bricks.

Most people post the floors on Instagram. They never show the foundation.

You don't need to broadcast every win.

Just keep stacking.

Let your net worth make the noise later.

———

🧭 WHY THIS MATTERS (AND WHERE IT FITS INTO THE BIGGER PLAN)

This chapter brings us back to the hard truth: money doesn't fix you. Habits do.

Every dollar you earn is either a brick for your structure or a crack in the wall.

The more you understand this, the faster you get free—not because you made a fortune, but because you built something strong enough to hold one.

That's how freedom happens.

You don't wait for the elevator to the top.

You build your own stairs.

And if your foundation is solid?

The zeroes will stack themselves.

———

💥 READY FOR MORE?

Remember you can't fix a weak foundation by stacking more bricks. And you can't fix bad money habits by adding more money. In fact, more income without structure isn't a solution—it's a setup. Because the cracks get bigger when the pressure increases.[8] Let's examine this in the next chapter.

———

📌 **FOOTNOTES & CITATIONS:**

Sources and citations for this chapter can be found in the back of the book under "Footnotes and Citations."

FOUR

WHEN MORE MONEY
MAKES THINGS WORSE

Why income alone won't save you if your foundation is fractured.

💡 **CONCEPT:**

More money doesn't fix broken systems. It feeds them.

Most people think more income will cure their financial problems. A raise. A new client. A surprise windfall. They treat it like financial medicine.

But here's the truth: if you don't have a structure, more money just pours into the cracks.[1]

We saw this in *Habits Beat Zeroes*—how your foundation, not your income, determines whether you can actually build. But this chapter goes deeper. Because once the money starts flowing, the real test begins.

The real danger isn't being broke. It's finally making good money— and still being stuck.

———

🧠 THEORY

Money is an amplifier. If your habits are unstable, your income just scales the chaos.[2]

We've been sold the dream that more money automatically equals more freedom. That if we just "got our money up," everything else would follow.

But money doesn't create discipline. It reveals the lack of it.

It doesn't replace systems. It exposes how weak they are.

Here's what that looks like in real life:

You make $70K and feel behind.

You hit $100K and still feel behind.

You touch $200K—and your lifestyle explodes just fast enough to stay broke at a higher level.[3]

The outside looks different: better clothes, nicer car, bigger apartment.

But the stress? The juggling? The pressure? Still there. Worse, even.

Because what's been upgraded is the price tag—not the process.

———

❌ MYTH VS. ✅ REALITY

❌ **Myth:** "Once I earn more, I'll finally be able to get ahead."

✅ **Reality:** More income magnifies whatever system you already have. [4]

Think about this: a business doesn't become more organized just because it earns more revenue. If anything, it becomes more chaotic—unless the backend is rock solid.

Same with your life.

If your current setup doesn't include:

- Clear tracking of income and expenses
- Purpose-based priorities (not just vibes and mood)
- Margin between your lifestyle and your income
- Regular review of what your money is actually doing

- Then more income just means more speed, more pressure, and more room for error.
- It's not about income. It's about structure.

Real-life examples:

- The new six-figure earner who never upgraded their budget—still using the same old spreadsheet (if that). Now, the consequences of mistakes are bigger.
- The small business owner who adds new clients but never hires help. Burnout arrives just in time to ruin the best quarter of the year.
- The freelance creative who lands three big gigs but forgets to save for taxes—and ends up with the IRS in their inbox.

None of these people have an income problem. They have a system(s) problem.

———

📊 ACTION PLAN

Before you earn more, upgrade how you manage what you already have.

Let's walk through a mini-framework to stop money from making things worse:

A. 👉 Audit Your Foundation

Before more income hits your account, run this systems check:

- Do you know where your money goes weekly?
- Do you have a spending structure—automated or manual—that actually reflects your real life?
- Are your goals broken into clear targets, or are they vague, emotion-based wishes?
- Do you have breathing room, or is every dollar already spoken for?

- This isn't about being perfect. It's about being prepared.

B. 👉 Pre-Decide the Next Tier

Write down exactly what you would do if you earned:

- $1,000 more per month
- $5,000 more per month
- A one-time $25,000 windfall

Give every dollar a job—before it even arrives.
That one shift alone turns chaos into clarity.[5]

C. 👉 Protect the Gap

The single most powerful indicator of wealth isn't income—it's margin.[6]
The space between what you make and what you spend.
When your expenses rise at the same speed as your income, you're just climbing a treadmill in better sneakers.
Build the habit of resisting immediate lifestyle upgrades just because more money is available. Instead, expand your cushion first. Buy time before you buy things.

D. 👉 Build in Reset Points

Every 90 days, do a systems reset:

- What income came in?
- What did I keep?
- What changed about my goals or needs?
- Did I actually make progress, or just look busier?

This short cycle keeps growth intentional.
Without it, most people sprint in circles.

———

WHY THIS MATTERS

Because the truth is: bad math and poor systems cost more than low income ever will.[7]

This is where the next chapter—*Money Math for Real Life*—steps in. Because if you don't understand how margins, percentages, and time-value math actually work, you'll fall into the same trap at every income level.

We'll unpack that next.

But first, take this to heart:

Just because you're earning more doesn't mean you're growing.

And just because something looks like success doesn't mean it's sustainable.

You don't need more money.

You need a structure that won't collapse when more money finally arrives.

And here's one more layer most people miss:

Not all money is created equal.

A new client might bring in $3,000 in a month... but is it **Blue money**? (A salary) **Teal money**? (Self-employment?)

Or is it **Purple money** (accounts receivable—money in theory, but illiquid)?

Maybe even **Black money**—a lump sum from a tax refund. One-time money, not to be mistaken for stable income.

This is where knowing the "color" of your money matters most.[8]

We'll talk more about those income types in Chapter 19, *The Colors of Money™*—a full breakdown of how to think in financial categories that go beyond just dollars and cents.

But for now, lock this in:

If your foundation isn't strong, even "good" money can wreck your life.

So before you ask for more—ask if you're ready.

———

💥 READY FOR MORE?

The most perplexing place to be isn't broke—it's earning well and still stuck. And nowhere is that trap more visible than in the lives of so-called "high earners."

Big salaries. Fancy titles. Bigger problems.

This isn't freedom—it's a lifestyle illusion.

Let's examine this in the next chapter.

———

📌 FOOTNOTES & CITATIONS:

Sources and citations for this chapter can be found in the back of the book under "Footnotes and Citations."

FIVE

THE MYTH OF "HIGH INCOME"

Why a big paycheck ≠ financial freedom.

💡 CONCEPT:

Schools taught us to aim high—get the degree, land the six-figure job, climb the ladder. They did not teach us what that "high income" lifestyle really costs—or how often it leads right back to financial stress, just in a better zip code.[1]

———

🧠 THEORY:

There's a myth buried in the American dream: that if you make more money, you'll automatically be free. But the truth is, most high earners just buy more expensive cages.

You don't outgrow money problems by making more. You outgrow them by shifting your mindset, adopting better habits, and staying accountable to the principles that work—over time.

If you don't, lifestyle creep will enter. Each raise triggers a reward.

Bigger car, better neighborhood, private school, designer clothes. You're still stuck in the same cycle—just now you're playing it on hard mode.

This is where the golden handcuffs come in. You're living well, but not living free.

It's not the income that traps people. It's the unconscious assumptions about what success must look like.[2]

———

❌ MYTH VS. ✅ REALITY

❌ **The Myth:** "If I can just get to six figures, I'll be good."

✅ **The Reality:** Over 40% of people earning over $100K live paycheck to paycheck. Among those making $250K or more, about 36% report the same.[3]

Doctors. Lawyers. Tech executives. Many of them still feel behind. Because no one taught them how to keep or grow what they earned—only how to earn it.

Meanwhile, teachers and tradespeople with smart systems, intentional choices, and strong boundaries sometimes end up with more cash in the bank than their high-earning peers.

Money ≠ Mastery.

———

📊 ACTION PLAN

Here's how to break the myth:

- 👉 **Track your wealth, not just your income.** High earners often confuse gross pay with net gain. Focus on what you keep and grow.
- 👉 **Anticipate lifestyle creep.** Make conscious choices before

the raise hits. Where will the extra go? Automate it toward assets, not upgrades.

- 👉**Define freedom before you chase status.** What does your financial peace look like? Write it down. You can't buy freedom by accident.
- 👉**Uncouple ego from earnings.** A number won't validate your worth. Design a system that works for your life, not your LinkedIn.

———

🧭 WHY THIS MATTERS (AND WHERE IT FITS INTO THE BIGGER PLAN)

This is the hard truth: income alone doesn't change your financial life. Only your behavior, your systems, and your self-awareness do.

You don't need to make $200K to be free. You need to stop chasing the idea that higher income is a magic wand. That myth keeps good people broke.

This is the same game at every level—just with fancier packaging. If you learn to win while you're earning modestly, you'll scale that same discipline as you grow.

That's wealth. That's power. That's what they didn't teach you in school.

———

💥READY FOR MORE?

The illusion of "making it" often hides just how close someone is to financial collapse.

But the numbers don't lie. There are people earning six figures and still living paycheck to paycheck? That's not success; it's financial stagnation in disguise.

If that is you, you're in danger. Let's expose and help you save yourself with the next chapter.

———

📌 FOOTNOTES & CITATIONS:

Sources and citations for this chapter can be found in the back of the book under "Footnotes and Citations."

SIX

A HIGH EARNER GOING NOWHERE?

Why a strong salary with no structure is a financial death trap in disguise.

💡 CONCEPT:

If you earn more than $80,000 a year but your money isn't going anywhere, you're in more danger than you realize.[1]

I know this book isn't about budgeting. But this chapter? This is the exception to the rule.

Because here's the truth:

High income without asset acquisition is just an expensive treadmill.

You're running hard. Maybe even uphill. But you're not moving forward—because the treadmill was designed to keep you in place.

And worse? Your treadmill is one power outage away from stopping altogether.

———

🧠 THEORY:

The trap of high income is comfort.

You've got nice things. Your rent or mortgage is higher. Your wardrobe

27

is clean. You may drive something impressive. You take vacations. You eat out.

You feel like you're doing well.

But you're living on **Blue Money**. Salary money. Labor money. Time-for-dollars money.

And Blue Money is the most fragile color of them all.

Because when you're salaried, you don't control the faucet—your employer does.

Corporate America is in the business of cost-cutting, restructuring, and automation.

The higher your salary, the more incentive they have to replace you with someone younger, cheaper, offshore—or AI.[2]

High earners are always in the crosshairs.

You don't want to start making lifestyle changes when your income drops.

You want to do it now—while you still have the upper hand.

🤔 WHAT MOST PEOPLE GET WRONG

You think because you earn well, you're doing well.
But here's what most high earners never do: **buy income.**
They spend Blue Money like it's Green. But they never stop to ask:

- What have I actually built with this?
- Where is the income-generating structure?
- Could I survive three months without this job?

A six-figure salary with no assets is financial purgatory.

It feels like winning—until it's gone.

And when it's gone, you'll be looking around at the handbags, the sneakers, the nights out, the Uber rides, the streaming subscriptions, the overpriced rent...

And wondering what you really have to show for all of it.

👀 The Warning Signs

You're a high earner going nowhere if:

- You don't know how much you spent last month
- You couldn't survive more than 30 days without your salary
- You've never owned income-producing assets
- You tell yourself "I'll invest when I make just a little more"
- You've normalized spending 80–90% of your paycheck

Sound familiar? Don't beat yourself up.
But don't stay here.

✨ The Opportunity

Here's the great news:
You're in a position most people would kill to be in.
Unlike someone making $30,000 a year, you don't have to flip your way up from zero.
You can save your way to a passive income structure—you might even be able to buy one outright.
You could:

- Save $25,000 to $50,000 for a down payment on a cash-flowing property
- Buy an income-producing vending machine route
- Fund a low-overhead online business that runs without you
- Create an info product based on what you know
- Invest in Orange Money flips that produce real capital gains[3]

You can build the very thing most people only dream of—income you don't work for.
But only if you stop wasting your best shot.

———

📊 ACTION PLAN

A. 👉 Cut your lifestyle by 50%.

Yes—fifty. It sounds aggressive, because it is.

If you're spending $6,000/month, you need to get it to $3,000 and bank the rest.

Not because you're broke.

But because that surplus is your freedom fuel.

B. 👉 Create a Passive Income Fund.

Open a separate account.

Name it: "Freedom Fund," "Green Path," or "Asset Acquisition."

Every single month, that surplus goes here. No exceptions.

C. 👉 Map Your Escape Plan.

Choose a strategy. Pick your structure:

- Real estate rental
- Automated business
- Cash-flowing intellectual property
- Dividend portfolio

Decide which one you'll fund—and reverse-engineer the number.

You're not dreaming anymore.

You're designing.

———

🔄 THE MINDSET SHIFT

This isn't punishment. It's positioning.

You've been given the gift of a strong income—but the window may not stay open forever.

If you're a high earner, you're either funding your freedom—or financing your trap.

Your goal is to turn Blue Money into Yellow or Green—through Orange.

And to do that, you have to get real with your numbers.

Stop playing defense.

Use your current income to play aggressive offense—now.

Because one day that salary will end.

And when it does, you don't want to look back and say:

"I had it all... and I bought nothing that could save me."

———

💥READY FOR MORE?

Once you realize income isn't everything, a new anxiety creeps in—the fear of falling behind. Of missing out. Of not "growing" fast enough.

But growth without control is chaos.

And comparison is a thief that steals your strategy.

Let's examine it in the next chapter.

———

📌 FOOTNOTES & CITATIONS:

———

Sources and citations for this chapter can be found in the back of the book under "Footnotes and Citations."

———

SEVEN
CONTROL VS. GROWTH

Why You're Not Missing Out

💡 CONCEPT:

There's a panic that creeps in when you scroll your feed or talk to your co-worker who just started "maxing out their Roth IRA." When someone mentions compound interest, index funds, or that they "got in early," it can feel like you've already lost.

You start thinking, Damn… am I too late? Did I mess up by not starting a 401(k) at 22?

This fear is real. And it's everywhere. It's baked into headlines, money apps, and even your bank's sales pitch. But here's the truth:

You're not behind.

You're not missing out.

You're just playing a different game—and if you play it right, your growth can outpace theirs. But first, you need control.

———

🧠 THEORY:

Control Is More Powerful Than Early Compounding—When You're Broke

Compound growth is beautiful—but only when there's something to compound.[1]

If you're living paycheck to paycheck, dodging overdraft fees, and can't cover a $400 emergency without panic, then investing in a low-return, long-term vehicle is not the answer. Not yet.

Because right now, your #1 asset isn't the market—it's your control.

- Control over your income.
- Control over your expenses.
- Control over your decision-making window.
- Control over your ability to pivot when life hits.

People often say "time in the market beats timing the market." That's true—for people with money.

For you? Gaining control over your money, your systems, and your mindset is the most valuable investment you can make.[2]

———

❌ MYTH VS. ✅ REALITY

"Early Is Everything" vs. "Leveraged Control"

❌ **The Myth:** If you don't start investing for retirement in your 20s, it's over. You'll be 65, broke, and regretting every Starbucks you ever bought.

✅ **The Reality:** What actually derails people's wealth isn't late investing. It's a lack of control for too many years. No buffer. No plan. No muscle.

That's what keeps people broke in their 30s, 40s, and even 50s.

What if you took 24 months to gain total control? To master your cash flow, kill off bad debt, build your capital skills, and start small flips that generate quick income?

You could leapfrog over someone who's been putting $200/month into a retirement account since college and still doesn't know how to manage a budget.

Early money grows, yes. But aggressive, controlled money multiplies.

Your timeline might not be slow and steady. It might be compressed and strategic.

That's the real power of leveraged control: it lets you bend the rules of the traditional game.

———

ACTION PLAN: TANGIBLE STEPS TO RECLAIM FINANCIAL CONTROL

Let's break it down into 5 power moves:

1. 👉 **Master Your Cash Flow (Weekly Wins)**

Set a weekly money meeting with yourself. Know what's coming in, what's going out, and what you're choosing to ignore. Control starts with awareness.

Don't wait until the 30th to find out your rent is short.

Tactical Tip: Use the Weekly Flow Check-In:

- What money did I make this week?
- What did I keep?
- What am I avoiding?

2. 👉 **Build Your Parachute**

This is your short-term safety net. Start with $1,000 for emergencies, then stack a second layer for car and life repairs.

Control doesn't mean avoiding chaos—it means not crashing when it hits.

"You can't grow what you can't hold on to."

3. 👉 **Reduce or Replace Red Money**

Credit card debt, predatory loans, past-due bills—these kill your control.

Prioritize small capital flips (reselling, freelance gigs, odd jobs) and use 100% of that money to pay down Red.

Every dollar you take back from debt is a dollar you control again.

4. 👉 Build Your Orange Muscle (Small Flips, Fast Gains)

Start generating capital gains money on the side. Not huge flips—small ones. T-shirts, digital services, appliances, used phones.

Practice the cycle: buy smart, sell fast, reinvest.

This money isn't just income—it's *training*.

5. 👉 Protect Your Time & Decision Window

When you're broke, you're on someone else's clock.

Control means buying time—enough buffer that you can choose your next move instead of reacting.

"The goal isn't just money. It's breathing room."[3]

———

🖍 EXAMPLE:

Imagine two people, both 30 years old:

- Person A contributes $200/month to a 401(k). They have $3,000 in savings and $8,000 in credit card debt.
- Person B uses the next 24 months to pay off all their debt using flips, builds a 3-month emergency fund, and starts earning $500/month from a side hustle they now control.

By age 32, who has more options?

Who's less panicked during a job loss?

Who's positioned to invest with confidence, not fear?

The answer isn't about Wall Street. It's about control.

———

🧭 WHY THIS MATTERS:

Control Comes First in the Bigger Wealth Plan

In this book, we're building a stacked system—a methodical climb from survival to freedom.

And every stage has a primary goal:

- ⚪ **White Money** protects you. 🛡️
- 🟥 **Red Money** undermines you. 🪤
- 🔵 **Blue Money** covers basics. 🧾
- 🟠 **Orange Money** gets you moving. 🔄
- 🟡 **Yellow Money** starts paying you back. 💸
- 🟢 **Green Money** sets you free. 🕊️

But all of that depends on how much control you have.
Because without control, the rest falls apart.

Control is how you move with confidence.
Control is how you spot opportunity and act fast.
Control is how you build wealth—not in theory, but in real life.

This isn't about rejecting growth. It's about sequencing it.
Control is your launchpad. Growth is what happens next.

———

🔔 FINAL REMINDER:

You're not late.
You're not behind.
You're not excluded.
You're just starting from a place that demands strategy, not shame.
And control? That's the most strategic move of all.

———

📌 FOOTNOTES & CITATIONS:

Sources and citations for this chapter can be found in the back of the book under "Footnotes and Citations."

EIGHT

SACRIFICE IS SACRED

Choose work while others sleep, so you can one day sleep while others still have to work—for someone else's benefit.

💡 CONCEPT:

Sacrifice isn't punishment. It's power. It's not about loss—it's about building the life you actually want.

Most people misunderstand sacrifice. They think of it as deprivation. As a kind of suffering. But sacrifice isn't about pain for the sake of pain—it's about purpose. It's what builds the foundations of financial independence. What looks like a detour is often the only path to real wealth.

And here's the truth: you will sacrifice either way. The only question is for whose benefit? You can sacrifice your time and freedom for someone else's vision—or you can direct that sacrifice toward your own.

———

 **THEORY:**

"You'll never be great at anything for which you are not willing to sacrifice."

– DR. MAYA ANGELOU

That quote hit me so hard, I still remember where I was when I heard it. She said it in passing during an interview. It wasn't even the focus of the conversation, but the line carved itself into my memory. I have no idea what else she said that day—but that stuck.

Because it's true.

If you want financial freedom—true independence, not just surviving paycheck to paycheck—then sacrifice isn't optional. It's sacred.

Marketing has tricked us into believing we should have more than we're willing to earn. That ease is the goal. That effort means something is broken. That's false conditioning. Ease is the reward, not the route.

You want to reach the top? That takes focus. That takes work. And it takes giving up what's comfortable now for what matters most later.

✖ MYTH VS. ✅ REALITY

✖ **Myth:** Sacrifice means suffering, loss, or failure.

✅ **Reality:** Strategic sacrifice is the most powerful leverage you have. It's how you buy freedom—on your terms.

You don't get to skip sacrifice. But you do get to choose its purpose.

If you don't make deliberate, intentional sacrifices for your future, you'll make unconscious, repeated sacrifices for someone else's.

📊 ACTION PLAN

You're already making a sacrifice by reading this book. That counts.
But here's how to keep going:

- 👉 **Monitor your mindset.** Doubt will creep in. Monitor it.
- 👉 **Stick to systems.** Let habits carry you when motivation doesn't.
- 👉 **Trade short-term comfort for long-term power.** That might include weekends, vacations, and even some relationships.
- 👉 **Cut distractions.** You can't build your future in the presence of people who don't believe in futures.
- 👉 **Work in silence.** Let results speak for themselves. Gain momentum before inviting feedback.
- 👉 **Adjust constantly.** Life will throw wrenches. So what? Adjust. Learn. Keep it moving.
- 👉 **Respect the process.** Every dollar needs a purpose. Every hour needs a reason.

———

🧭 WHY THIS MATTERS (AND WHERE IT FITS INTO THE BIGGER PLAN)

Sacrifice is the price of ownership. Ownership of your time. Ownership of your money. Ownership of your outcomes.

You are not just budgeting dollars. You are budgeting effort. Focus. Hours. Relationships. Environment. Beliefs. All of it.

People think money is the hard part. It's not. Discipline is.

But if you've made it this far, you're already proving that you're different. That you're ready. That you understand what most people will never grasp: this journey takes everything—but it gives you back even more.

This isn't punishment.

It's not loss.

It's not lack.

It's sacrifice.

And sacrifice is sacred

———

📌 FOOTNOTES & CITATIONS:

Sources and citations for this chapter can be found in the back of the book under "Footnotes and Citations."

NINE

THIS ISN'T A 401(K) BOOK...

And Why That's Exactly the Point

"Retire at 65? That was the dream they sold your grandfather when gas was 40 cents a gallon. This book is about building real wealth in 5 to 15 years — not waiting 40."

💡 CONCEPT: 401(K) THINKING VS. FREEDOM THINKING

They told you to get a job, contribute to your 401(k), and ride it out until retirement. Maybe, if the market doesn't tank and you live long enough, you'll get to enjoy a few years of travel and golf — if your knees still work.

That's the default plan.

But that's not your plan.

This book isn't anti-401(k). It's anti-delay.

This book is about creating real financial independence in years, not decades. We're after income you control, not just balances you can't touch until you're too tired to care.

You want freedom now, not just security later. You want your money to work for you long before you're 65. And that requires a different blueprint.

———

🧠 **THEORY:**

Why Traditional Retirement Planning Falls Short

Let's break down the truth behind the 401(k) system and why it's not your primary tool here:

- **It's built for slow growth — and slow freedom.** You contribute small amounts monthly and wait 30–40 years, hoping for compounding to kick in. The returns can be solid — if you have decades.
- **You can't access it without penalty until 59½.** That means no matter how disciplined you are, your reward is delayed by design. No flexibility, no exit ramp.
- **It's passive in the worst way.** You hand over control to market cycles, financial advisors, and HR departments. There's no real leverage. You're just a quiet passenger on a slow train.
- **It's tied to a job.** Most 401(k)s live inside company-sponsored plans. If your goal is to exit the job system in the next 5–10 years, why would your main plan be tied to it?
- **It wasn't designed for now.** The 401(k) is a boomer-era vehicle for boomer-era jobs and boomer-era costs. It wasn't built for freelancers, flippers, digital income, or fast-scaling entrepreneurs. It assumes you want to be an employee until the end. That's not your path.

None of this makes the 401(k) useless — it just makes it secondary. A backup parachute. Not your primary plane.

———

❌ **MYTH VS.** ✅ **REALITY**

❌ **MYTH:** "If you don't max out your 401(k), you'll never retire."

✅ **REALITY:** If you only max out your 401(k), you might never live.

Freedom doesn't come from balance sheets alone — it comes from cash flow you control. From building assets now that generate income while you sleep. From systems you own, not salaries you chase.

There are people who've flipped vending machines, digital assets, or rental arbitrage deals into five-figure monthly incomes. And none of that came from a brokerage statement.

You don't need 40 years.

You need a system, a plan, and 12–24 months of relentless focus.

———

📊 ACTION PLAN

A. Focus on Cash Flowing Assets, Not Just Long-Term Holdings

Your goal is income — monthly, scalable, semi-passive.
- ✅ Vending machines
- ✅ Domain flipping
- ✅ Digital content with royalties
- ✅ Short-term rentals
- ✅ Service businesses with systems

These are orange-to-yellow money plays (see: *The Colors of Money™*). They build skills, capital, and then income streams. They don't require waiting until you're 60.

B. Use Capital Gains to Buy Time, Not Just Things

When you flip a product, service, or small business deal — don't blow it. Don't use that $1,200 profit for shoes. Use it to knock out debt. To cover a month of expenses. To fund your next flip.

The first time your capital gains cover your phone bill, your mindset shifts. The first time they cover rent? You'll never see money the same way again.

C. Build Systems to Turn Work Into Passive Assets

If you're self-employed, great. But if you're still doing everything, it's a job with a different boss: you.

The pivot is to turn your hustle into a system — something others can help run, something that generates income without you having to show up every time.

☑ Document your process
☑ Automate part of it
☑ Train someone else
☑ Detach from daily operations

That's how blue money (job income) becomes orange (capital gains), then yellow (passive income).

D. If You Do Use a 401(k), Treat It Like Insurance

Sure, go ahead and contribute enough to get your company match — that's free money.

But don't obsess over it—don't make it the centerpiece of your plan.

Use it like a long-term emergency parachute — not your life vest.

E. Plan for a 5–15 Year Freedom Runway

This book is written for people who want to exit the rat race in 5 to 15 years. Not fake retire. Not grind quietly. Exit.

That means stacking active cash-flow skills in your 20s, 30s, 40s, or even 50s so that by your next decade, you own your time.

That's the game.

And it's very, very winnable.

———

🧭 WHY THIS MATTERS (AND WHERE IT FITS IN THE BIGGER PLAN)

The school system didn't prepare you for this. And neither did most financial advisors.

That's not because they were evil — it's because their system rewards safety and compliance. Your system requires clarity, courage, and capitalism.

Your life doesn't need to follow the old formula:
"Get a job, fund a 401(k), hope for a retirement party with sheet cake."

You can build a system that buys your time back.
You can use your salary to fund flips.
You can turn flips into passive assets.
And you can turn passive assets into real wealth.

This isn't a book about someday.
It's about sooner than you think.

And that's why this isn't a 401(k) book.

———

💥 READY FOR MORE?

The old blueprint said to wait decades for a return. We're not doing that. You're not just here to save—you're here to build. And to build anything meaningful, you need more than motivation. You need mechanics. Structure. Systems. Let's examine it in the next chapter

———

📌 FOOTNOTES & CITATIONS:

Sources and citations for this chapter can be found in the back of the book under "Footnotes and Citations."

TEN

FIRST, THE PARACHUTE

You Can't Grow What You Can't Hold On To

💡 CONCEPT:

Investing without savings is like jumping out of a plane with no parachute.

You might enjoy the view for a while—but when things go wrong, you've got nothing to slow the fall. That first $1,000 in cash savings isn't just a soft landing. It's your defense. It's your timing. It's the one thing that keeps your investments from getting yanked before they mature. And the second $1,000? That's your patch kit—the backup for the breakdowns life throws your way.

———

🧠 THEORY:

People often think savings and investing are interchangeable financial strategies. They're not. Investing is about growth; savings are about survival. Without survival, your growth never gets to finish growing.

That's why you don't just need a savings buffer—you need a two-tier system:

- **Tier One**: General emergency savings to keep you breathing.
- **Tier Two**: Targeted savings for the two places life hits hardest —cars and homes.

This structure gives you time, power, and options. And time, in the world of wealth, is everything.

———

❌ MYTH VS. ✅ REALITY

❌ **Myth**: "Saving money is for cautious people. I'd rather grow my money by investing."

✅ **Reality**: Without savings, you'll never keep what you grow.

Too many new investors—even smart ones—skip the savings step in an effort to "make up for lost time." But that impatience creates fragility. A single emergency can force you to sell off assets too soon, missing the gain entirely. Savings are what allow you to wait—and wealth rewards the ones who can wait.

———

📊 ACTION PLAN

Start with **Tier One**: $1,000 in general emergency savings.

This is your "do not touch" buffer—your personal parachute. It keeps you from liquidating assets every time life throws a curveball.

Next, build **Tier Two**: another $1,000—split like this:

- $500 for car expenses
- $500 for home or life expenses

This second tier covers the two emergencies that hit the average person the most—and the fastest. It's small, but strategic. You'll be shocked how often this exact breakdown shields your investments from early withdrawals.

Once both tiers are funded, you're cleared to invest:

- Your own small business
- A flip (car, collectibles, property—see chapter: *Small Bucks, Big Gains*)
- Short-term stock or crypto plays
- Any asset you've studied that aligns with your goals

And even then—you keep growing your emergency cushion alongside your investments.

Because power doesn't just come from growth—it comes from being able to wait.

————

⊘ WHY THIS MATTERS (AND WHERE IT FITS INTO THE BIGGER PLAN)

This chapter solidifies the foundation you built in *Seeds and Fruit*. That chapter taught you how to spot the difference between what you plant and what you harvest. This chapter shows you how to keep your seeds in the ground long enough to actually grow something.

Skipping savings is a rookie move with expensive consequences.

Having savings? That's the play that separates hustlers from strategists.

This is what it means to play the long game—and actually win it.

Saving isn't sexy, but it's what keeps you alive when the market turns or life hits hard. Still, the moment people save a little, they rush to invest—too soon, too fast. But just because you're no longer falling doesn't mean you're ready to fly. Sometimes, sitting still is the smartest move you can make.

————

💥READY FOR MORE?

Let's explore the topic a bit deeper. In the next chapter: *When You Shouldn't Invest (Yet).*

📌 FOOTNOTES & CITATIONS:

No citations required. Financial perspectives presented reflect the author's framework for accelerated wealth-building and do not constitute individualized financial advice.

ELEVEN

WHEN YOU SHOULDN'T INVEST (YET)

And Why That Pause Could Actually Be Your Power Move

💡 CONCEPT:

Sometimes the smartest move in the money game... is to sit still. Not forever—but for long enough to build your base. That pause isn't weakness. It's strategy. Because investing when you're financially or mentally unready can be the fast track to losses, fear-based decisions, and broken momentum. This chapter gives you full permission to stop and steady your foundation first—without guilt.

———

🧠 THEORY:

The personal finance world often pushes one mantra: "Start investing early." And yes, time in the market matters—but what's rarely said out loud is that your position before you invest matters even more.

The person who throws $1,000 into an index fund while panicked, broke, and one car breakdown from a disaster isn't investing from strength. They're gambling from stress.

The person who invests from a place of calm clarity, even if they start later, is usually the one who wins.

This book isn't anti-investing. It's pro-readiness.

You're building something different here. You're not relying on a 40-year grind and hoping it grows. You're taking command of your timeline—sometimes aggressively, sometimes patient. This is one of those patient moments.

———

❌ MYTH VS. ✅ REALITY

❌ **MYTH:** "If I'm not investing right now, I'm losing."

✅ **REALITY:** If you're not ready to invest—because you're still rebuilding your emergency savings, paying off bad debt, or learning how money actually works—then NOT investing right now might be the smartest wealth decision you'll ever make.

What you're doing instead is building the system that can handle real wealth when it comes.

The people who lose in investing? They didn't start too late. They started without a plan.

They pulled out early. Got scared. Chased trends. Ignored fees. Copied social media hype.

All because they didn't have the foundation this book is walking you through.

So breathe. You're not late. You're just strategic.

———

📊 ACTION PLAN: FIVE SIGNS YOU SHOULD WAIT BEFORE YOU INVEST

A. 👉 **You don't have a buffer.**

Test question: Could you cover a $1,000 emergency without touching your investment account?

If not, you're not ready. Every dollar you invest must be a dollar you can afford to leave alone. Otherwise, you'll pull it out at the worst time.

👉 **What to do instead:**

Stack up your white money (savings) until you've got at least two tiers:

- Tier 1: $1,000 core buffer
- Tier 2: Situation-specific reserves (home, car, security cushion)

B. 👉 **You're carrying high-interest debt.**

If your credit card is charging you 22% interest, no stock on earth is going to "outperform" that in a reliable way.

👉 **What to do instead:**

Use capital gains flips (orange money) to knock down red money (debt) first.

Freeing up that monthly interest is a guaranteed return on investment.

C. 👉 **You don't understand what you're investing in.**

"I heard it was a good stock" is not a strategy. Neither is FOMO or TikTok hype.

If you don't know what a company does or how a rental property cash flows, it's not time.

👉 **What to do instead:**

Use this time to study. Watch a few Warren Buffett interviews[1].

Read a breakdown of dividend investing. Play mock investment games[2].

I think smart, well-designed investment games are one of the most underrated habit-building tools out there—which is why I'm developing my own. (Join our email list so you'll get first notice when it's ready.)

Do all your mistakes on paper first.

D. 👉 You're emotionally attached to fast results.

If the market drops 10% and you panic-sell? That wasn't investing—it was gambling.

You must be willing to play the long game. That requires emotional bandwidth, not just money.

👉 **What to do instead:**

Focus on your internal game. Practice delayed gratification with small things first.

Start a 30-day challenge: No unnecessary spending, no checking the market.

Learn to control your impulses before the stakes are high.

E. 👉 You don't have a system.

Wealth without a system falls apart.

If you don't know how you'll track gains, pay taxes, or rebalance, it's not time yet.

👉 **What to do instead:**

Build the system: a Money Day routine, percentage breakdowns by color (remember Blue–Orange–White–Red), and automation setups.

Even if you're not investing yet, you're preparing like a pro.

———

🧭 WHY THIS MATTERS (AND WHERE IT FITS INTO THE BIGGER PLAN)

Pausing to prepare isn't stepping back. It's pulling the bowstring.

And it will launch you further.

By taking 12 to 24 months (or up to 36 depending on life), you are:

- Developing financial reflexes instead of reacting emotionally
- Creating cash flow strategies that are layered and flexible
- Learning to earn your way into the market, not fumble into it
- Protecting your investments with buffers and backups
- Honoring the simple truth: Your account, your control, your confidence.

If you follow the steps in this book, you will start seeing tangible results within 12 months. That might be your first vending machine paying you weekly.

Your first flipped product funding your emergency savings.

Your first month where passive income covers groceries.

By 24–36 months, if you stay focused, your passive streams should start catching up to your core expenses.

From there? That's freedom math.

This chapter is your permission slip to pause.

Not out of fear—but out of power.

Because investing is a chapter, not a starting point.

And you? You're writing the whole book.

Let's make the next chapter count.

If you're ready to shift gears, go re-read *Small Bucks, Big Gains*.

If you're not there yet, re-read *The Parachute*.

And when you're ready to flip orange gains into yellow income, you'll know.

———

💥 READY FOR MORE?

Once you learn to pause, you see how many financial moves are made from pressure, not power. The next lie to confront? That you're "saving" just because you bought something on sale. The game doesn't change until you realize: keeping money beats spending less of it. Let's examine it in the next chapter.

———

📌 FOOTNOTES & CITATIONS:

Sources and citations for this chapter can be found in the back of the book under "Footnotes and Citations."

TWELVE

SPENDING AT A DISCOUNT IS NOT SAVING

Why "sales" are not savings—and how marketing stole the word.

💡 CONCEPT:

You didn't *save* $20 when you spent $80 on a "discounted" item.

You spent $80.

True savings only happens when money stays with you—not when it's redirected to a merchant's register.

Let's be clear:

A discount is not savings unless the discount lands in your White Money.

Otherwise, it's just a price cut dressed up as a financial virtue.

———

🧠 THEORY

The word "savings" used to mean something powerful.

Security. Reserve. Safety. Future.

Then came decades of retail marketing.

Coca-Cola, Macy's, Target, Amazon—they've all poured **millions** into blurring the line between **spending less** and **saving more**.

Now, the term "Save $10 Today!" is stamped across receipts, ads, coupons, emails, shopping apps—even when it leads you into spending more than you intended.

Buy-One-Get-One.

Two-for-Tuesday.

Flash Sales.

"Exclusive Member Savings."

These aren't savings. These are **psychological triggers**.

The average person has been so manipulated, they now believe:

Putting money aside to **spend later** is saving.

Getting a discount off an inflated retail price is saving.

Buying more than they need to "save per unit" is logical.

*They've rebranded spending as saving—**and you've been paying for it.***

What's Really Happening

Let's break it down.

If you walk into a store to buy one pair of socks for $10...

But you see a "Buy 2, Get 1 Free" sale, and spend $20 instead of $10...

Did you save? No.

You **spent more** than you planned in pursuit of imaginary savings.

Yes, you got more product.

Yes, the "unit cost" went down.

But unless you had a need for that volume—and had budgeted for it—this was a manipulation.

And you fell for it.

Now imagine that same $10 went to your White Money—your emergency reserve, your dry powder.

That's real savings. That's money **retained**, not redirected.

The White Money Standard

Let's revisit The Colors of Money™:

🟢 Green = Second-gen passive income
🟡 Yellow = First-gen passive income
🟠 Orange = Capital gains
⚪ **White = Savings**

White Money is your **cushion**, your **margin**, your **self-insurance**.
It's what prevents a car repair or a dental bill from becoming a crisis.
And every time you tell yourself you "saved" by spending less—but never moved that saved amount into White Money—you lost an opportunity to build security.
Savings don't count until they're captured.

———

⊘WHY THIS MATTERS

The dangers of confusing discount with savings:

You spend more chasing the illusion of value.
Discounts incentivize purchases you wouldn't have made.

Bulk deals overstock your home and undercut your budget.
You never build the habit of true saving.

You become a reactive buyer, not a proactive planner.
Your White Money stays empty.

And when life hits—and it will—you're unprepared.

The Correction: A Simple Practice

Here's how to reclaim the word "savings":

Step 1: Name your White Money account.
Give it emotional meaning:
"Peace of Mind Fund"
"Life Cushion"
"Buffer Fund"
"I Don't Panic Money"

Step 2: Every time you "save" money at a discount, match it.
If you were going to spend $40 and got it for $30?
Put the $10 difference into that account.
Every single time.
Don't just calculate it—**transfer it**.
Otherwise, it's nothing more than mental accounting.

Step 3: Learn to walk away.
If a sale requires you to spend more than you intended, it's not a deal—it's a trap.
Learn to be okay with buying one instead of three. Or none instead of one.
Be okay with sitting a sale out.
White Money is built through restraint, not coupons.

Shift Your Identity

People who accumulate real wealth are not coupon-chasers.
They're not retail-deal addicts.
They are **money reallocators**.
They **redirect** spending into strategic buckets—like capital growth (Orange) and security (White).
Let others brag about how much they saved at the mall.
You'll be busy building cash reserves, buying assets, and controlling outcomes.

Final Word:
If the money didn't reach your White Money account...
You didn't save it.
You just spent it at a discount.

Real savings are quiet, powerful, and yours to keep.

Build them with intention—not imaginary markdowns.

So much of what we're taught is about spending smarter. But what if the real advantage comes from not spending at all? Liquidity—having cash ready, flexible, and fast—isn't just a financial metric. It's a mindset shift. One that gives you choices when others are stuck.

———

🔔 FINAL WORD:

If the money didn't reach your White Money account...
   You didn't save it.
   You just spent it at a discount.
   Real savings are quiet, powerful, and yours to keep.
   Build them with intention—not imaginary markdowns.

———

💥 READY FOR MORE?

Most of the advice out there is about spending better. But what if the real edge comes from not spending at all? Liquidity—having cash ready, flexible, and fast—isn't just a financial metric. It's a mindset shift. One that gives you choices when others are stuck. Let's examine it in the next chapter.

———

📌 FOOTNOTES & CITATIONS:

Sources and citations for this chapter can be found in the back of the book under "Footnotes and Citations."

THIRTEEN

THE PSYCHOLOGY OF LIQUIDITY

How access to cash—or the lack of it—shapes your decisions, your risk tolerance, and your entire financial identity.

💡 CONCEPT:

Liquidity means access.

Not just how much money you have, but how fast you can move.
How fast you can say yes. Or no.
How fast you can leave. Or invest. Or protect yourself.

Cash is speed.
Cash is control.
Cash is power—**but not because it buys stuff.**
Because it **buys you time and better options.**

———

🧠 THEORY:

Most people don't realize they're making life decisions from a place of panic, restriction, or delay.

Not because they're unintelligent.

Not because they don't want to win.

But because they're trying to solve permanent problems from temporary states.

And liquidity—**even a small amount**—can flip your entire perspective.

A person with access to $2,000 in flexible liquidity (cash, savings, credit, a trusted friend) makes very different choices than someone with zero cushion and a car on E.

When you have no liquidity, every decision gets filtered through **urgency.**

When you have liquidity, every decision gets filtered through **strategy.**

Same brain.

Different access.

Radically different life.

———

❌ MYTH VS. ✅ REALITY

❌ **The myth:** *"If I had more money, I'd feel more secure."*

✅ **The reality:** It's not about *more money.*

It's about *available money.*

It's about being able to access $500 on a random Thursday when the tire blows.

Or $5,000 when an opportunity shows up that expires in 48 hours.

Or $50,000 when the market dips and everyone else is panicking.

Liquidity is what turns knowledge into action.

Without it, even smart people stay stuck.

———

ACTION PLAN:

Let's get specific. Liquidity means:

Cash (in a savings account you don't touch for lunch money)

Credit (responsibly maintained credit cards, lines of credit, or business credit)

Cash equivalents (assets you can liquidate in 72 hours or less—stocks, bonds, crypto, etc.)

Trustworthy access (a parent, partner, friend, or business relationship you could lean on temporarily—only if needed)

Now, here's your plan to build a **Liquidity Shield**:

Step 1: Your "No-Matter-What" Number

Set your first liquidity goal. This is money you do not touch unless your life depends on it.

Recommended start:

$500 for vehicle breakdowns

$500 for home, life, or travel emergencies

$500 for unexpected opportunities

Total: **$1,500–$2,000**

This is your first layer of real freedom. Not wealth—**freedom.**

Step 2: Guard It Like a Pitbull

This liquidity is not for vacation.

Not for shopping.

Not for rent unless you're about to be homeless.

This is **sacred stability.**

Because when people have **no liquidity, they panic.**

And panicked people make dumb choices with long-term costs.

Step 3: Expand It

Once you've built your basic shield, expand it to fit your income bracket and lifestyle.

$5,000 = Breathing room
$10,000 = Power plays become available
$25,000 = You can fire a boss or buy a small asset
$50,000 = You become a buyer when others are frozen
Very Advanced Tier:
$50,000–$100,000 in pure liquidity—**from Green Money only.**
This isn't beginner money. This is legacy money.

This is **catastrophe mitigation cash.** The money you never touch unless everything hits the fan.

Think lawsuits, pandemics, major market crashes, unexpected family emergencies.

The money that makes sure one disaster doesn't erase 15 years of progress.

Step 4: Protect It from Your Own Ego

Liquidity feels powerful.
So it's easy to start flexing.
To treat your own cushion like a buffet.
That's how broke habits return with a fresh fade.
Don't let access turn into arrogance.
Discipline is what makes liquidity a weapon.
Ego is what makes it a leak.

———

💥READY FOR MORE?

Liquidity buys you options—but only if you've made yourself a priority. And most people don't. They pay everyone else first—the landlord, the bank, the bills—then hope something's left over. Flip that. Because wealth doesn't wait for leftovers. Let's examine it in the next chapter.

———

📌 FOOTNOTES & CITATIONS:

Sources and citations for this chapter can be found in the back of the book under "Footnotes and Citations."

FOURTEEN

PAY YOURSELF FIRST ISN'T JUST A SAYING

Why the richest people treat themselves like a bill—non-negotiable.

💡 CONCEPT

You've heard it before: pay yourself first.

But schools never broke down what that actually means—or why most people don't do it.

It's not about selfishness.

It's about survival.

It's about sovereignty.

Before you pay rent, the light bill, or even that overdue credit card, you set aside something for your future self.

Not because you have extra—but because you won't ever have extra until you do.

———

🧠 THEORY

Most people operate in reverse.

They get paid, cover expenses, and try to save what's left.

But what's left is usually zero.
And when savings is optional, it disappears.
Paying yourself first flips the psychology.
It turns wealth-building into a fixed cost—like rent.
You're telling the universe (and your nervous system): *I matter enough to fund.*
Even if it's $10.
Even if it's $2.
This isn't about the number.
It's about the identity.
Savers save because they decide to.
Not because it's easy.

————

❌ MYTH VS. ✅ REALITY

❌ **The Myth:** "I'll save once I have more wiggle room."

✅ **The Reality:** If you don't start now, more money won't help.

The habit builds the future, not the amount.

Studies show that people who automatically save—even small amounts—accumulate significantly more over time than those who wait to "feel ready."[2]

Why?

Because automation removes willpower from the equation.

It turns a wish into a system.

Most people fail not because they don't want freedom—
but because they've never built a system for it.

————

📊 ACTION PLAN

Here's how to make it real:

👉**Set a flat number**, not a percentage—at first.

- If 10% feels overwhelming, start with $25 a check. Start real. Then scale.

👉**Automate it.**

- The moment your money lands, a slice should move to savings or investing—before you touch it.
- No emotion, just math.

👉**Treat it like a bill.**

- If you wouldn't skip rent, don't skip this.
- Your future is the most expensive thing you'll ever owe.

👉**Name your buckets.**

- Emergency fund. Freedom fund. Investment fund.
- Labeling gives your savings purpose—and purpose fuels momentum.

———

🧭 WHY THIS MATTERS (AND WHERE IT FITS INTO THE BIGGER PLAN)

This isn't about stashing pennies in a jar.

It's about reclaiming agency.

When you pay yourself first, you shift from survival to strategy.

You stop being a leftover.

You stop hoping there will be enough.

You become the priority.

Financial freedom doesn't start with income—

It starts with respect.

This is your first move.

Every other chapter in this book builds on it.

💥 READY FOR MORE?

Paying yourself first is powerful—if you actually understand what you're keeping.

The problem? Most people think in earnings, not margins.

They talk about income, not profit.

Let's clean up the math and terminologies, so you can start counting what really counts.

📌 FOOTNOTES & CITATIONS:

Sources and citations for this chapter can be found in the back of the book under "Footnotes and Citations."

FIFTEEN

MONEY MATH FOR REAL LIFE

Making sense of percentages, margins, and why most people miscalculate wealth.

💡 CONCEPT: IF YOU CAN'T COUNT IT, YOU CAN'T KEEP IT

Most people are doing math... just not the right kind.

They calculate how much they *make*.

They don't calculate how much they *keep*.

They count their salary, but forget taxes.

They track expenses, but ignore margins.

They brag about six-figure sales, but can't explain net profit.

They *think* they're building wealth, but they're just spinning numbers that sound good.

Real wealth isn't what you earn—it's what you keep, what you grow, and what you control.

This chapter is about cutting through the noise and learning the math that actually

Matters.

———

🧠 THEORY:

Financial Freedom Isn't a Feeling—It's a Formula

Money is emotional—but money **freedom** is mathematical.

If you don't understand percentages, margins, and basic return math, someone else will do the math for you—and profit off your confusion.

Here's the truth:

You don't need calculus. You don't need a finance degree.

But you *do* need a few core numbers burned into your brain—numbers that tell you whether you're moving forward, standing still, or bleeding out.

Emotions lie. Percentages don't.

———

❌ MYTH VS. ✅ REALITY

"I Make Good Money" vs. "I Keep Good Margins"

❌ The Myth: Income Equals Success

A $100,000 job.

A $50,000 side hustle.

A six-figure Shopify store.

These sound impressive... until you zoom in.

That $100K job might be $67K after taxes.

That $50K hustle might be $48K in *costs* and $2K in stress.

That Shopify store might have 9% profit margins—meaning $9K take-home after $100K in sales and $91K in overhead.

But here's what most people do:

They only post the gross numbers.

They only feel the top line.

They never calculate the *truth*.

✅ The Reality: It's All About Margins, Retention, and Leverage

A small income with a high margin can outperform a big income with zero leverage.

You make $30/hour freelancing. Great. But how many hours are you billing? And how many are unpaid admin work?

You flipped a couch for $200 profit. Even better. How much time, gas, and effort did that really cost?

You own a business that brings in $5K/month. But if you're working 60 hours and netting $1K, that's a job in disguise.

If you don't calculate your *true margin*—time, money, energy, and freedom—you'll keep chasing vanity numbers that never free you.

📊 ACTION PLAN: LEARN THE REAL MATH THAT BUILDS FREEDOM

Let's break this down into usable formulas and mental checkpoints.

1. Know Your Take-Home: Salary vs. Net Pay

The Math:

If you earn a $100,000 salary, don't get comfortable saying "I make six figures."

After taxes, Social Security, Medicare, and other deductions, your real take-home is closer to **$67,000–$72,000** depending on your location.

What to Do:

Calculate your *actual* monthly take-home. Not your salary. Not your gross income.

Then work backwards from *that* number to build your budget and investment plan.

2. Understand Profit Margin

Profit margin = (Profit ÷ Revenue) × 100
Let's say you sell $1,000 worth of baked goods in a weekend.
But you spent $600 on supplies, packaging, booth fees, and gas.
Your profit = $400

Your margin = (400 ÷ 1000) × 100 = **40%**

Now let's say your friend runs a Shopify store that made $10,000 this month, but spent $9,100 on ads, inventory, and software.

Their margin = **9%**

What to Do:

👉 Stop asking "How much did you make?"
👉 Start asking "What was your margin?"
👉 Margin is truth.

Margin is where freedom lives.

3. Calculate Time Leverage

Let's say two people both earn $5,000/month.

Person A works 10 hours/week using digital products and automation.

Person B works 60 hours/week fulfilling custom orders.

Who's freer?

Answer: The one with **time leverage**.

Time leverage ratio = Income ÷ Hours worked

It's not a sexy Instagram stat, but it'll change your life.

Time is your most expensive currency. Don't forget to count it.

4. Use Return on Investment (ROI) for Decisions

ROI = (Net Return ÷ Cost of Investment) × 100

Let's say you spend $200 on a domain name.

You flip it for $800.

Net Return = $600

ROI = (600 ÷ 200) × 100 = **300%**

That's strong. And that kind of flip matters more than a 2% raise at work.

———

👉 WHAT TO DO:

Use ROI to assess everything—tools, ads, flips, learning, even side hustles.

If it's draining time and money without real return, it's not an investment. It's a **leak.**

5. Learn the Colors of Your Money *(Expanded)*

Not all money is the same—and when you learn the difference, you move smarter. I use a system I created called ***The Colors of Money™***. It helps you identify not just where your money is coming from, but what it's meant to do.

Here's a quick breakdown:

Savings (White): This money's job is to protect your time and decisions. It's not for investing. It's your parachute. It buys you breathing room when life hits hard.

"You can't grow what you can't hold on to."

Salary Money (Blue): This is the conservative, stable money you use to pay bills, build a buffer, or slowly fund long-term investments. It's earned by renting your time.

"Stability before style."

Debt Money (Red): Borrowed money, not yours. Its only role is to create leverage—for capital or passive income—but only when you know what you're doing.

"Move fast, be surgical."

Entrepreneurial Money (Teal): You own the work, but it still owns you. This is the money made from side hustles or businesses where you're still trading effort. It can be powerful, but it's not yet passive.

"Transitional freedom with work still required."

🟠 **Capital Gains Money (Orange)**: Flip money. Trade something for more than you paid—resell, invest, build value. This is the muscle-building zone.

"Transition tool—bridge to assets or debt payoff."

🟡 **Passive Income Gen 1 (Yellow)**: Your first taste of freedom. Cashflow you don't clock in for, but that still needs reinvestment and care.

"Don't break the machine before it scales."

🟢 **Passive Income Gen 2 (Green)**: True freedom. This is your exit plan. Systems, real estate, investments, royalties—income you could walk away from without the engine dying.

"This is the goal. But earn it with intention."

⚫ **Windfalls & Wildcards (Black)**: Lottery money, crypto spikes, sudden checks. Fast money needs slow planning or it disappears. Use it to launch your long-term plan, not chase a fantasy.

"Launch wealth plan, not fantasy."

If you want to go deeper into this system, I've got a whole book in the works called **The Colors of Money™**—sign up for my list to be first to know when it drops.

👉 WHAT TO DO:

Track not just your income, but what *color* it is.

Aim to shift slowly from red to yellow to green.

Green and blue money are where freedom gets built.

 WHY THIS MATTERS: STRATEGY BEATS SALARY EVERY TIME

People get caught in emotional math:

"I work hard, so I *deserve* this."

"If I just made $20K more, I'd be good."

"I make good money—I'm fine."

But if you don't understand margin...

If you don't calculate leverage...

If you don't track what *sticks* versus what *spends*...

You'll stay broke with a good income.

You'll stay tired with a good hustle.

You'll stay dependent with a "business."

This chapter is your wake-up call.

Because the people who win at money?

They don't always earn more.

They just *know their numbers*—and use them like weapons.

———

🔔 FINAL WORD: FREEDOM IS A MATH GAME—PLAY TO WIN

Don't let anyone tell you money is just only about mindset.

Mindset is step one.

Math is step two.

The money game isn't just about effort. It's about **intelligent multi-plication**:

Multiply margin

Multiply leverage

Multiply time

Multiply returns

And subtract distractions, bad deals, and ego-fueled expenses.

You don't need to become an accountant.

But you *do* need to stop guessing—and start calculating.

Track it.

Understand it.

Then play offense.

Because when your math is sharp, your future is clear.

💥 READY FOR MORE?

Once you know how to count right, one truth slaps you in the face: someone else is already taking a cut—before you ever touch your check. His name is Uncle Sam. And if you're on the employee path, he's your biggest, most silent expense.

📌 FOOTNOTES & CITATIONS:

1. The Colors of Money™. Developed by the author, Robyn La'More, is a proprietary financial framework that categorizes income types by risk, leverage, and wealth-building potential. Explanation in Chapter 19 School Didn't Teach You This. The Colors of Money™ Robyn La'More. All rights reserved.

SIXTEEN

UNCLE SAM, YOUR SILENT PARTNER

The Tax Code Targets Employees First & What You Can Do About It.

 **CONCEPT:**

If you earn all your money from a job, you have a silent partner in every paycheck.

His name is Uncle Sam—and he takes his share before you ever see yours.

Most employees don't understand how aggressively they're taxed because it's done automatically, invisibly. They just know they work hard and still feel behind. This chapter reveals why—and how to begin reversing it.

———

 **THEORY**

The U.S. tax system appears progressive. But in critical ways, it's regressive—especially for people who earn money through labor instead of assets or business ownership.

- Earned income is taxed first, taxed most, and taxed without options.
- Laborers are taxed before they can save, invest, or deduct.
- Asset holders and business owners—on the other hand—can grow money first, then pay taxes later, often at lower rates.

Your income stream determines your tax strategy.
If all your income is Blue Money, your hands are tied before you start.

❌ MYTH VS. ✅ REALITY

❌ **Myth:** "If I work harder, I'll get ahead."

✅ **Reality:** If you work more hours, you just give Uncle Sam a bigger slice.

Even with well-meaning tax changes like overtime exemptions, you're still getting hit:

- Payroll taxes (Social Security & Medicare) don't go away.
- FICA taxes only apply up to $168,600[1]—but after that, higher earners stop paying.
- Your employer's "share" of your payroll taxes? It usually gets factored into your total compensation—which means you're really carrying the cost.

And the biggest myth of all?

Myth: "Everyone pays their fair share."

Reality: The tax code isn't fair. It's structured. Structured for ownership.

Structured for those with passive income, assets, or businesses—not just jobs.

📊 ACTION PLAN

You don't need to become a tax expert. But you must stop being a tax victim.

Here's how you shift from taxed-on-labor to taxed-on-leverage:

- 👉 **Track your income sources by color.**

If everything you earn is Blue Money, you're exposed. Diversify.

- 👉 **Start a Teal Money stream (entrepreneurial income).**

Even a small side business opens up powerful tax deductions:

- Home office
- Travel
- Meals
- Software and tech
- Business education and development
- These aren't loopholes. These are tools—built for business owners.
- 👉 **Graduate into Orange, Yellow, and Green Money.**

Use capital gains (Orange) to buy or build income streams that shift your tax position entirely.
The moment you earn before taxes, you've changed the game.

- 👉 **Learn the numbers.**

Understand the FICA cap. Understand deductions vs. credits.
Stop guessing and start planning.

- 👉 **Stop waiting for refunds.**

Your goal is not a bigger refund. Your goal is a smaller taxable footprint.

———

🧭 WHY IT MATTERS

If you rely only on labor, you will always be taxed the hardest and helped the least.

The IRS doesn't reward grind. It rewards structure.

This is why:

- The rich get richer.
- The self-employed have write-offs.
- The asset-holders grow wealth with lower taxes.
- And traditional employees stay stuck—working more and keeping less.

But this isn't the end of the story.

When you restructure your income sources...

When you shift from Blue to Teal... and eventually Yellow or Green...

When you start leveraging the same tax code written to benefit business owners and investors...

You stop being the underdog. You stop bleeding money.

You start playing offense.

———

🔔 ONE LAST THOUGHT

The IRS wasn't built for working-class people.

It was built by those who understood structure—for those who could afford to.

But now you know. And when you know the rules, you're not trapped in the game.

You're rewriting it.

📌 FOOTNOTES & CITATIONS:

---

1. *The Colors of Money™. Developed by the author, Robyn La'More, is a proprietary financial framework that categorizes income types by risk, leverage, and wealth-building potential. Explanation in Chapter 19 School Didn't Teach You This. The Colors of Money™ Robyn La'More. All rights reserved.*

SEVENTEEN

THE ASSET ADVANTAGE

How the Tax Code Rewards Ownership Over Labor

 **CONCEPT**

You've been told that working hard pays off. But when it comes to taxes, the U.S. tax code pays ownership—not effort.

Employees are taxed early and automatically. Owners get options, advantages, and time.

Assets—not hours—create the real wealth.

———

 **THEORY**

The tax system is not broken. It works exactly as designed.

It's not a tool for equality—it's a blueprint for incentivizing certain behavior: job creation, housing development, business expansion, and capital investment.

When you align your financial habits with the behaviors the tax code rewards, the system begins to work for you instead of against you.

That's the Asset Advantage.
You don't need to be rich to use it.
You need to be intentional.

———

❌ MYTH VS. ✅ REALITY

MYTH: "Everyone pays their fair share."
✅ **REALITY:** The rich pay less by design, not deception.

MYTH: "Taxes are what you owe for earning money."
✅ **REALITY:** Not all money is taxed the same—assets are taxed less.

MYTH: "You have to be rich to benefit from the tax code."
✅ **REALITY:** You just need to own income-producing assets—even small ones.

———

✅ ACTION PLAN

1. Learn the Power of Capital Gains

Long-term capital gains (profits from selling assets held over a year) are taxed at 0%, 15%, or 20%—often far lower than salary income.[1]
👉 *Start small: stock apps, fractional shares, or buy-and-hold crypto and real estate.*

2. Understand Depreciation

When you own a rental property or income-generating equipment, you can claim depreciation.
That means cash flow stays high, while taxes stay low.
👉 *Begin exploring real estate education or investing in REITs to learn.*

3. Respect the Order of Operations

Employees: **Earn → Taxed → Spend**
Business owners: **Earn → Spend → Taxed**
👉 *Launch a small business or monetized side hustle. Even small income earns tax advantages.*

4. Borrow Smart

The wealthy borrow against appreciated assets rather than sell them—no taxes triggered.
👉 *As your assets grow, consider low-interest credit lines on property or brokerage accounts (wisely).*

5. Build to Flip or Hold

Buy assets with the goal to either:

- Flip for capital gains (Orange Money), or
- Hold for cash flow (Yellow/Green Money).

Either way, you're exiting the all-labor economy—and entering the owner's economy.

———

💥 WHY IT MATTERS

The system isn't going to change to reward your labor more fairly.
The game is rigged in favor of ownership.
This isn't about cheating the system. It's about understanding it.
And finally using it.
You don't have to make millions to benefit from these principles.
You just have to own something. Anything that makes money without trading time for dollars.
One vending machine.
One ebook.

One rental room.
One long-held stock.
These are seeds.
And each seed is taxed differently than your labor.
That's not a loophole. That's architecture.

———

✨ ONE LAST THOUGHT

The tax code is the government's blueprint for behavior.
    If you act like an owner, you'll be taxed like one.
    If you act like an employee, you'll be taxed early and often.
    Start small.
    Grow strategically.
    Shift intentionally.
    The reward isn't just lower taxes.
    It's freedom.

———

💥 READY FOR MORE?

The tax code didn't evolve by accident. It was built—rigged—to reward those who own and penalize those who trade time for money.
    So don't just complain about the system. Learn it. Play it. Master it.
    Then flip the whole board. Let's examine it in the next chapter.

———

📌 FOOTNOTES & CITATIONS:

No citations required. Financial perspectives presented reflect the author's framework for accelerated wealth-building and do not constitute individualized financial advice.

EIGHTEEN

THE GAME IS RIGGED—SO LEARN TO PLAY

Why mastering the rules lets you flip the board

💡 **CONCEPT:**

Everybody says it—*"The system is rigged."*

And you know what?

They're right.

But that's not the end of the sentence. It's the beginning of a challenge.

The game is rigged.

So learn the rules. Study the rigging. Master the mechanics. Then flip the damn board.

This chapter is not about victimhood.

This is about power.

Systemic power. Strategic power. Psychological power.

The game is built on rules. Some written. Some whispered.

And if you're willing to learn how the game works—not just how it looks—you'll stop being a piece on someone else's board.

You'll become a player. Maybe even the one who builds the next board.

School didn't teach you this.

But the system did. Loudly. Through who wins. Through who owns. Through who gets to walk away while others carry the weight.

The rich don't guess.

The rich **leverage, structure, and own**.

And if you want to join the table, you don't have to wait to be invited.

You need to **learn the rules, break them if you must, and reframe them in your favor**.

———

🧠 THEORY:

The system isn't random.

It isn't fair—but it *is* predictable.

And predictability is power.

Wealth is not an accident.

It's the result of **strategy**. The stacking of tools—**ownership, leverage, access, timing, and protection**.

If you're losing, it's not because you're dumb.

It's likely because you were taught a different set of rules.

You were taught to be a worker.

To trade hours for dollars.

To avoid risk.

To worship job security over ownership.

Meanwhile, the winners were taught how to:

Borrow money to make money

Use corporate structures to reduce taxes

Buy assets and hold them

Pay people smarter than them

Protect wealth in trusts and LLCs

Leave instructions, not just inheritance

You don't need to copy their lives.

But if you're serious about breaking generational cycles, you *must* study the game.

You must stop playing emotional checkers on a strategic chessboard.

❌ MYTH VS. ✅ REALITY

❌ **Myth:** "If the system is rigged, there's no point trying."

✅ **Reality:** *If* the system is rigged, there's *every* reason to try—strategically.

Complaining that the game is unfair but refusing to learn how it works is like watching a poker table from the parking lot and being mad you never win.

The truth is that *most people lose* because they never learn the rules.

They think working harder will change the scoreboard.

But hard work without strategy is martyrdom.

The system is not here to save you.

But that doesn't mean you can't save yourself by outsmarting the system.

The more you learn about **money, credit, asset protection, income types, taxation, depreciation, business law, and negotiation**, the harder you are to exploit.

This chapter isn't about "becoming rich" for flex.

This is about becoming **so fluent in the game that your kids aren't pawns**.

📊 ACTION PLAN

Here's how to start playing the rigged game like a strategist:

1.👉 Learn the Tax Code Like an Entrepreneur.

The IRS doesn't just punish; it rewards. Business meals, home office deductions, travel.

You can legally lower your tax burden. But only if you stop thinking like an employee.

2. ☞Stop Earning Solely From Labor.

If your only income is earned income (W-2, 1099), you're taxed at the highest rate.

Start building income from assets—rental property, small businesses, capital gains.

3. ☞Use Entities for Leverage and Protection.

LLCs and S-Corps aren't just for show. They allow separation, write-offs, scalability, and insulation.

4. ☞Study Trusts and Estate Planning.

Wealth is preserved through planning, not through willpower.

A family trust can change everything. You don't have to be ultra-rich to set one up.

5. ☞Learn the Language of Leverage.

Poor people avoid debt.

Rich people *optimize* it.

There's toxic debt, I call it red money (personal credit cards used for consumer debt) and there's tool debt, I call that bronze money (business debt used for real estate, business expansion). Learn the difference.

6. ☞Surround Yourself With Game Players.

You cannot win the game if everyone around you thinks the board is imaginary.

Find people who think bigger. Who own things. Who talk structure and equity instead of side hustles only.

7. ☞Practice Strategic Thinking Every Day.

Before any financial move, ask:

- What are the rules here?
- Who actually benefits from this offer?
- Am I an owner or a customer in this transaction?
- Is there a smarter structure I'm not seeing?

———

🧭 WHY THIS MATTERS (AND WHERE IT FITS IN THE BIGGER PLAN)

This was not designed as the first chapter for a reason.

Before you can appreciate *why* the game is rigged, you need to understand *what* you're trying to build.

This chapter is a pivot point.

This is the moment when you stop reacting emotionally to the unfairness, and you start **studying it like a future architect**.

The system may be rigged.

But once you understand the levers and pulleys, it becomes hackable.

You don't fight it by shouting.

You fight it by creating *your own damn board*.

And if you're serious about money—not just surviving with it, but weaponizing it for freedom—this mindset is non-negotiable.

You're not just learning finance.

You're learning **financial warfare**.

And the first rule of war is: *Know the terrain*.

The rich know the rules.

And now?

So will you.

———

💥 READY FOR MORE?

Now that you've seen behind the curtain, it's time to build your own structure. Not just to survive—but to scale. Mastery begins when you stop reacting to the system and start designing your own.

———

📌 FOOTNOTES & CITATIONS:

Sources and citations for this chapter can be found in the back of the book under "Footnotes and Citations."

NINETEEN

THE COLORS OF MONEY

Why Every Dollar You Touch Needs a Job—and a Color

🔥 **Sneak Peek from Upcoming Book: *The Colors of Money*™**

This chapter introduces my proprietary visual money system, designed to help you *see* and *use* money by mission. Each Color follows a seed-to-fruit pathway. If you like this chapter, you'll love what's coming next.

 CONCEPT

All money spends the same—but not all money *is* the same.

One of the most dangerous myths in personal finance is the idea that all dollars are equal just because they have equal spending power. But the truth is: some dollars are seeds. Others are fruit. Some build. Some destroy. And until you learn to categorize each dollar by its *source*, *purpose*, and *timeline*, you will always be fighting against invisible currents.

That's why I created The Colors of Money™ system[1].

———

🧠 THEORY

This system helps you assign a job—and a purpose—to every dollar you touch. By assigning a **color** to each major type of money you encounter (salary, debt, passive income, capital gains, windfalls, etc.), you create a filter for emotional and financial discipline.

You'll stop spending seed money on luxuries. You'll stop using debt as income. You'll stop treating credit like cash. You'll start thinking in phases—from Red (debt) to Green (freedom).

Each color represents a mission. Each mission supports the next.

———

❌ MYTH VS. ✅ REALITY

❌ **MYTH:** "Money is money. It doesn't matter where it comes from—just get enough of it."

✅ **REALITY:** Money is like medicine. The wrong kind at the wrong time will kill your momentum. Credit is not the same as salary. Salary is not the same as capital gains. Capital gains are not the same as passive income. Confusing these categories leads to debt spirals, lifestyle traps, and long-term financial paralysis.

———

📊 ACTION PLAN: THE COLORS AND THEIR RULES

Here's a first look at the core Colors of Money—a system I built through years of research, real-life trial and error, and practical application. It's not magic, and it's not foolproof—but it *works*. If you take the time to learn it, it will shift how you see, use, and grow money—and build wealth.

🔴 RED – DEBT MONEY

Borrowed money: credit cards, personal loans, consumer debt.

Purpose: Temporary comfort for long-term pain. Often used to rent a lifestyle you can't afford.

☞**Action Rule:** Eliminate it. Use Orange or Teal Money to pay it off with urgency.

Mindset: This is *not* your money. It comes with interest. It benefits the lender. Treat it as an emergency, not a convenience.

🔵 BLUE – SALARY MONEY

Earned income from a job or W-2 labor.

Purpose: Stability. Covers rent, bills, essentials, and emergency prep.

☞**Action Rule:**

70% Essentials (housing, bills, food, starter savings)

20% Long-term investments (IRAs, index funds, etc.)

10% White Money (tiered emergency savings)

Mindset: Use Blue to survive, not to stunt. Build safety, not style.

🔷 TEAL – ENTREPRENEURIAL MONEY

Profits from businesses you actively work in. You own the work, but the work still owns you.

Definition: Transitional freedom, still labor intensive.

Purpose: Ownership with effort.

☞**Action Rule:**

30% Reinvest into the business

30% Fund flips to generate Orange Money

20% Taxes

10% Lifestyle upgrades (direct pay only—no down payments)

10% Into White Money (until 1 year of expenses is saved)

Reminder: Teal is powerful, but it's not passive. Use it to graduate into passive income.

🟠 ORANGE – CAPITAL GAINS MONEY

Money earned through flips, small investments, side hustles, or asset sales.

Purpose: Capital growth or debt elimination.

☞**Action Rule:**

80% Toward asset-building or Red Money payoff

20% Taxes

Mindset: This is your financial gym. Build muscle here. Flip wisely, and you'll earn your way to freedom.

🟡 YELLOW – PASSIVE INCOME (GEN 1)

Rental income, royalties, dividends, business distributions. Money that flows without your daily effort.

Purpose: Begin measured lifestyle upgrades and reinvestment.

👉**Action Rule:**

30–40% Lifestyle

50–60% Reinvestment into more passive income

Goal: Passive income ≥ total debt + your aspirational lifestyle

Mindset: Yellow feels freeing—but it's fragile. Reinvest before relaxing.

🟢 GREEN – PASSIVE INCOME (GEN 2)

Reinvested Yellow Money that produces consistent income with high autonomy.

Purpose: True financial freedom.

👉**Action Rule:**

70% Lifestyle freedom and time choice

20% Reinvestment

10% Philanthropy, legacy, or long-term expansion

Mindset: You made it. Now sustain it. You don't reach Green by accident—you build it, one color at a time.

⚫ BLACK MONEY– WINDFALLS & WILDCARDS

Unexpected money: inheritance, lottery, settlements, surprise gifts.

Purpose: Jumpstart generational wealth—not fantasy lifestyles.

👉**Action Rule:**

50% Passive assets

40% Controlled upgrades or Orange investments

10% Mad Money (1-time, no payments)

Mindset: Windfalls disappear fast. Use the surprise to create something stable.

⬤ PURPLE MONEY – ASSETS IN WAITING

Money dependent on others: equity payouts, inheritances, partner-controlled ventures.

Purpose: Optional advantage—not a plan.

Mindset: Don't count it until it clears. But if it does—make it count.

⬤ White – Savings

Liquid reserves for emergencies—not investment.

Definition: Short-term protection money.

Purpose: Protection, not production.

Mindset: White Money isn't supposed to grow—it's supposed to shield your Orange and Yellow Money while you build.

⬛ BRONZE MONEY – BUSINESS CREDIT (SELF-LIQUIDATING DEBT)

Debt backed by income-producing assets—not by your labor or primary home.

Definition: Not "real" money—it's a credit instrument used responsibly.

Purpose: Use for properties or businesses where *others* repay the debt (renters, customers, etc.)

Rules:

Never exceeds 50% loan-to-value

Never used on personal-use property

Never over-leveraged without reliable, passive repayment

Footnote:

⬛ Red Money and ⬛ Bronze Money are *not real money*—they are debt instruments that spend like cash. Use with extreme caution.

💥 WHY THIS MATTERS

You cannot build financial freedom by treating all money as equal.

Color coding your money adds *clarity*, *discipline*, and *strategy* to your financial decisions.

You'll stop reacting emotionally.

You'll start moving with purpose.

And most importantly—you'll stop confusing effort with progress.

Once you see your money in color, you'll never go back to gray.

———

✨ READY TO GO DEEPER?

This was just the introduction.

In the upcoming book *The Colors of Money™: The Structure of Money (Making Money Make Sense)*, learn how to:

Identify what color dominates your life now

Transition income streams across the color spectrum

Mix money types for growth and protection

Apply color strategy in relationships, legacy planning, and more.

🎯 Want tools, templates, and strategy maps?

Join the waitlist at **TheColorsOfMoney.com** and unlock early bonuses

In the meantime...

———

💥READY FOR MORE IN THIS BOOK?

Once you learn to color your money, something shifts—you stop treating all dollars equally. But there's another trap hiding in plain sight: even when people recognize the value of their income, they keep spending what was meant to grow. Knowing the type of money is one thing. Knowing how to use it? That's the next level.

📌 FOOTNOTES & CITATIONS:

---

1. The Colors of Money™. Developed by the author, Robyn La'More, is a proprietary financial framework that categorizes income types by risk, leverage, and wealth-building potential. Explanation in Chapter 19 School Didn't Teach You This. The Colors of Money™ Robyn La'More. All rights reserved.

TWENTY

SEEDS VS. FRUIT

Stop Eating the Seeds

 **CONCEPT**

Seeds are for planting. Fruit is for eating.

But too many people are eating what was meant to grow.

———

🧠 **THEORY**

Money comes in different forms—and not all of it is ready to be spent. Some money is *seed money*: small, early-stage, high-potential capital meant to be **flipped, reinvested, or protected**. Other money is *fruit*: the outcome of growth—yields, profits, passive income.

The danger is in treating them the same.

If you eat your seeds, you'll never grow your fruit.

If you mislabel fruit as seed, you'll undernourish your life.

Knowing the difference is everything.

———

❌ MYTH VS. ✅ REALITY

❌ **MYTH:** "Money is money. If it's in my account, it's mine to spend."

✅ **REALITY:** The source of your money determines its destiny.

If it's a flip profit, it's a **seed**. Replant it.

If it's passive income from an asset, it's **fruit**. You can enjoy some.

If it's a one-time windfall, split it carefully between **planting** and **enjoyment**.

Most people *spend everything like it's fruit*. That's why they're always broke.

Smart builders reinvest. They delay the feast. They grow orchards.

———

📊 ACTION PLAN

1. 👉 Classify Your Income

Use The Colors of Money™ as a visual guide:

🟥 **Red 'Money'** is dangerous debt.

🟠 **Orange Money (Capital Gain Flips):** Seed

🟡 **Yellow Money (Passive Income):** Fruit

🟢 **Green Money (2nd Gen Passive):** Premium Fruit

🔵 **Blue Money (Salary):** Mixed (mostly operational, with some long-term seeds)

🔷 **Teal Money:** Earned through entrepreneurial efforts.(must be split)

⚫ **Black Money (Windfalls):** Hybrid (must be split)

⚪ **White Money = Savings**

🟫 **Bronze 'Money'** is credit that **self-liquidates.**

*🟥 Red Money and 🟫 Bronze Money aren't "real" money — they're debt instruments.

2. 👉 Set a "Seed Ratio" Rule

Every time you flip or earn in the early stages, commit:

→ 80% gets replanted into another flip or income asset
→ 20% is your "light" reward or held for taxes/safety

3. 👉 Resist Lifestyle Inflation

Do not upgrade your life with seed money. If you earn $500 flipping phones, do *not* go shopping. Flip again. Build. Earn the right to *use fruit money* to upgrade.

4. 👉 Create Your Seed Bank

Keep seed money visible but separate—psychologically and physically.

→ A high-yield savings account
→ A business reinvestment fund
→ A tax envelope
→ A Flip Again folder

This trains you to see **money as a tool**, not a treat.

———

🧭 WHY THIS MATTERS (AND WHERE IT FITS)

Your financial destiny depends less on how much you make and more on what you *plant* and what you *eat*. This chapter reinforces the principle of **discipline before freedom** and **growth before comfort**.

It sits at the heart of this book's entire message:

You're not here to spend money better.

You're here to use money differently.

Understanding *Seeds vs. Fruit* prevents the single biggest mistake people make when trying to build wealth: *eating the power before it multiplies.*

If you're ready to stop being a consumer and start being a grower, this is your pivot point.

———

💥 READY FOR MORE?

Once you stop eating your seeds, you realize just how many of your financial choices were built around short-term survival. School trained you to think in 30-day cycles. But the real players don't live by the month—they move by strategy. It's time to flip the calendar.

———

📌 FOOTNOTES & CITATIONS:

1. *The Colors of Money™. Developed by the author, Robyn La'More, is a proprietary financial framework that categorizes income types by risk, leverage, and wealth-building potential. Explanation in Chapter 19 School Didn't Teach You This. The Colors of Money™ Robyn La'More. All rights reserved.*

TWENTY-ONE

MONEY BY THE MOVE VS. MONEY BY THE MONTH

Why shifting from a monthly mindset to a moves-based framework unlocks real strategy.

💡 CONCEPT:

Money by the Month is how most people are trained to think.

Get paid. Pay bills. Rinse and repeat. It's a pattern—and a trap.

Money by the Move flips that script. It's strategic. Intentional. Purpose-driven. You start thinking like a boss, not a budget victim.

This is one of the clearest examples of something school didn't teach you. Why? Because most education systems train you to become a worker—someone whose entire financial world runs in monthly cycles. A 30-day treadmill. You're taught how to earn, not how to maneuver.

Switching to a *move-based mindset* is what separates short-term hustlers from long-term players.

———

🧠 THEORY

A monthly mindset is reactive. Your paycheck hits. You plug holes. You hold your breath until the next one. If an emergency pops up in Week 3? Panic. Swipe the credit card. You'll "figure it out" next month.

A moves-based mindset is proactive. You're not looking at the next 30 days. You're looking at your **next three money plays.** You build cushion, map the terrain, and time your actions based on leverage—not desperation.

This is how corporations operate.

They don't live month-to-month. They have quarterly reports. Year-end targets. Phased execution plans. They invest. Reinvest. Move assets around. Make data-based decisions.

They're not reacting to a phone bill. They're forecasting, pivoting, executing.

You have to become the **CEO of your own finances.**

❌ MYTH VS. ✅ REALITY

❌ **MYTH:** "I just need to make it through this month."

✅ **REALITY:** That mindset will have you *just making it* forever.

Most people think budgeting is about cutting back. But in the monthly loop, cutting back usually means cutting off growth. You're not trimming fat—you're starving your momentum.

You feel stuck because you're looking at life like a calendar, not a chess-board. You're trapped in a 30-day cash survival sprint.

And let's be honest: nobody wins marathons running 100-meter dashes back to back.

Switch to **moves-based thinking**, and suddenly, you have air. Space. Options.

You start asking different questions:

- "What's my next strategic move?"
- "Can I delay this purchase until it funds something bigger?"
- "How many moves away am I from cash flow freedom?"
- "What's my 90-day plan instead of my 9-day panic?"

You stop thinking in **bill cycles.**
You start thinking in **asset cycles.**
Growth cycles. Flip cycles. Tax cycles.
You build a whole new money operating system

———

📊 ACTION PLAN

Step 1: 👉Zoom Out.

Start asking: *What's my next financial move—not just my next paycheck?*
This could be:

- A small flip for $600.
- A new seed (side hustle) launch.
- A debt paydown move using a windfall.
- A network play that opens future doors.

Step 2: 👉Run the Numbers by the Quarter.

Instead of thinking in 30-day chunks, calculate where you want to be 90 days from now. Ask:

- What money do I want to move in or out?
- Which skills do I need to sharpen for the next opportunity?
- What phase am I in? *(Planting, watering, harvesting?)*

Step 3: 👉 Build an Opportunity Fund.

This is **NOT** an emergency fund.

This is a *play money* fund. Use it for:

- Buying undervalued assets
- Paying for coaching or mentorship
- Covering you while you make a strategic leap

Even $1,000 in green or yellow money, set aside for your next money move, can change your trajectory.

Step 4:👉 Create a 3-Move Map.

Draw it out. Literally.

- **Move 1:** Fix credit / save $500
- **Move 2:** Flip $500 into $1,200
- **Move 3:** Use $1,200 to buy inventory or launch digital product

That's a phase. That's strategy.
Now imagine stacking four of those in a year. **That's power.**

Step 5: 👉Change Your Language.

Stop saying:

✖ "This month's gonna be tight."
✖ "Let me just make it to payday."

Start saying:

✔ "My next move is to unlock $3K in cash flow."
✔ "I'm planting seeds right now for my Q4 goal."
✔ "This delay is part of my strategy."

That mental reframe alone will boost your decision-making IQ.

———

🧭 WHY THIS MATTERS (AND WHERE IT FITS INTO THE BIGGER PLAN)

You were trained to think paycheck to paycheck.

Even people with good salaries are trapped in that loop.

It's not about how much you make—it's about **how you move.**

When you shift to a **move-based model**:

✅ You stop fearing small delays
✅ You plan further ahead
✅ You allocate resources more intelligently
✅ You free yourself from the emotional chaos of paycheck living

Money is psychological.

And *money by the month* is designed to keep you anxious and compliant.

Money by the move puts you back in power.

This chapter is the pivot point.

Everything we've talked about so far—habits, Colors of Money, psychology of liquidity—was leading to this.

Now you have the mental model to build wealth *on purpose*.

One move at a time.

———

💥 READY FOR MORE?

When you start making money moves instead of monthly payments, you stop chasing checks and start building **structure.**

And *structure* is where the real power lives.

Hustle might get you paid.

But **systems?**

Systems get you free.

Let's examine that in the next chapter.

———

📌 FOOTNOTES & CITATIONS:

Sources and citations for this chapter can be found in the back of the book under "Footnotes and Citations."

TWENTY-TWO

SYSTEMS BEAT HUSTLE

Why the Hustle Won't Save You

 **CONCEPT:**

Hustle can get you out of the mud—but it can't build a bridge to long-term freedom. Systems do that. Consistency beats intensity. Whether you're freelancing, clocking in, or running a side hustle, the way to win is by installing systems that do some of the work *without* you.

———

THEORY:

Most people are taught to *work hard*. Few are taught to *design a system*. Hustle burns energy. Systems build engines. And engines run when you're tired, sick, sleeping, or scaling. You can't outwork broken math, leaky habits, or unsustainable effort.

Hustle is effort; systems are infrastructure.
Hustle is manual; systems are scalable.
Hustle depends on you; systems free you from being the bottleneck.

Hustle is temporary; systems are transferable.
Hustle helps you survive; systems help you grow.

————

❌ MYTH VS. ✅ REALITY

❌ Myth

"I just need to grind harder, and it'll all work out."

Truth: Most hustlers don't have a money problem—they have a *leak problem*. They're pouring time and effort into a container with no system to retain it. Working harder without a framework is like pouring water into a bucket with holes and expecting it to fill.

✅ Reality

You can hustle your way into burnout, not wealth.

Systems don't care how motivated you are—just whether they work.

Most successful people didn't just work hard. They tracked, tested, optimized.

The real wins are boring. Repetition, automation, review.

Motivation fades. Systems keep going.

————

📊 ACTION PLAN

👉 Track more than income.

Start with five core numbers: income streams, expenses, **consumer debt**, savings rate, and time allocation. Don't just look at how much you're making—**look at how you're making it**.

Build a rhythm.

Weekly money date. Monthly review. Quarterly goals. Don't leave your future to vibe and chaos.

Simplify inputs.

Choose 1–2 platforms, not 10. One solid savings method, not five apps. Get your process out of your head and onto paper.

Automate the obvious.

Bills, savings transfers, debt payoffs, donation tithes. What you don't automate becomes a leak.

Create feedback loops.

If something worked, why? If something failed, what broke? Systems aren't just routines—they're answers in motion.

———

WHY THIS MATTERS IN THE BIGGER PICTURE

This chapter is the foundation. Hustle might give you your first taste of wins—but systems determine if those wins are *repeatable*. Financial freedom is not about hype. It's about installing mechanisms that serve you even when you're tired. Even when you're distracted. Even when life hits.

This is how we go from survival to strategy.

From effort to elevation.

From hustling... to harvesting.

———

💥 READY FOR MORE?

You've heard the word "system" several times now. But what does that actually look like in the real world? How do people set up businesses and money flows that work even when they don't? Let's pull back the curtain on what freedom is actually built on.

———

📌 FOOTNOTES & CITATIONS:

Sources and citations for this chapter can be found in the back of the book under "Footnotes and Citations."

TWENTY-THREE

WHAT A SYSTEM LOOKS LIKE

 **CONCEPT:** *WHAT A SYSTEM LOOKS LIKE*

They didn't teach you this in school, but they should've: every institution you've ever interacted with—every company, every agency, every movement—is powered by a system. Not a person. Not a job. A system.

You were likely taught to specialize: become a nurse, a coder, a lawyer. But no one pulled back the curtain to show you *the system* that holds those roles together.

If you've ever wondered how CEOs seem to "do less" but earn more, or how some people scale businesses without burning out—it's because they understand systems. They don't just work inside them. They **build** them.

———

**THEORY:**

A System Is a Machine—Not a Person

At its core, a system is a repeatable process designed to produce consistent results. It includes:

Inputs (raw materials, people, ideas)
Processes (what happens to those inputs)
Outputs (results, revenue, services)
Feedback loops (data that helps you adjust)

This is true whether the system is your local coffee shop or Amazon. Systems are designed for two things:

Efficiency (less waste, more speed)
Scalability (can grow without collapsing)

Your job, your career, your business? All of it sits inside a system. If you don't see the system, you're just a cog. Once you learn to map it, you can manage it—or better yet, *own it.*

———

❌ MYTH VS. ✅ REALITY

❌ Myth 1: "I'm not a systems person."
✅Reality: If you can cook a meal or follow a routine, you already use systems. Systems aren't complicated. They're just steps that repeat—and that you can tweak.

❌ Myth 2: "Only big companies use systems."
✅ Reality: Every successful business, no matter how small, has systems. Your vending machine business needs a restocking system. Your resale hustle needs an inventory and shipping system. Systems don't mean employees. They mean *clarity.*

❌ Myth 3: "Self-employment is financial freedom."
✅ Reality: Owning your job is not the same as owning a system. If your business can't survive without you, you don't have a system—you have a second job. And that's still light blue income, not passive.

———

📊 ACTION PLAN: HOW TO SPOT THE SYSTEM IN ANY BUSINESS

A. 👉 Start with the Big Picture

Every system starts with an outcome. Ask:

What does this system exist to produce?

Who are the customers or end-users?

Example: A barber shop doesn't just cut hair. It delivers *consistent, scheduled service in a clean environment at an expected price.*

B. 👉 Identify Core Components

These are the parts almost all systems share:

Product or Service Delivery
What gets sold or done?
What tools or people are required?
Customer Acquisition (Marketing & Sales)

How do people hear about it?
What convinces them to pay?
Operations
Who does the work?
What are the day-to-day routines?
Back Office (Admin, IT, Finance)
How is money tracked?
How are systems maintained or optimized?
Communication Flows
How do people within the business stay aligned?
Where do instructions or decisions come from?

You may do all these roles yourself at first—but recognizing them helps you know *what* to replace when the time comes.

C. 👉 Study Expansion and Contraction

A real system doesn't collapse under stress—it adapts.

When demand rises, how does the system respond?
When it's quiet, what parts go into hibernation?

This is the magic of scalability: a good system expands without burning out the operator.

D. 👉Track the Human Roles Inside the System

In any business, people usually play one of five roles:

The Visionary – Sets direction (CEO/founder)
The Operator – Handles the day-to-day (manager)
The Technician – Does the actual work (worker/contractor)
The Marketer/Salesperson – Brings in money
The Accountant/Admin – Keeps the lights on

If you're just starting, you are *all five*. But don't worry. You won't stay there.

Why This Matters (and Where It Fits into the Bigger Plan)

If you ever want to stop trading your time for money, this chapter is the turning point.

Systems are what transform **income into assets** and **effort into equity**. You can't outsource chaos. You can only outsource a system. So if your long-term goal is to create passive income, generational wealth, or scalable businesses—understanding systems is non-negotiable.

Here's the deeper truth they didn't tell you in school:

Systems make success boring.
Boring is predictable. Predictable is scalable. Scalable is freedom.

So yes, you can hustle. Yes, you can flip. But if you want to walk away and still get paid?
Build the system.

———

💥READY FOR MORE?

Now that you've seen behind the scenes, it's time to build your own... system. Not a theory. A blueprint. Because if you're still doing everything yourself, you don't own a system—you own a job with extra steps.

———

📌 FOOTNOTES & CITATIONS:

Sources and citations for this chapter can be found in the back of the book under "Footnotes and Citations."

TWENTY-FOUR

HOW TO BUILD YOUR OWN SYSTEM

💡 **CONCEPT:**

The system is the difference between owning a job and owning a machine. Most people don't know the difference. That's why they stay stuck. A system takes you from *doing everything* to *delegating everything*, without the entire operation falling apart. A good system turns effort into output, time into leverage, and customers into cash flow—even when you're not in the room.

This is the chapter you'll return to. When you get stuck. When you level up. When it's time to make a move. Because this is where the blueprint lives.

———

🧠 **THEORY:**

A system is more than a collection of tasks. It's an interlocking structure of functions designed to move a specific result forward—on repeat. It's not about *how hard you work*, it's about *how smart your components work together*.

A great system will:
Handle complexity without chaos.
Scale without burning you out.
Make delegation clear and repeatable.
Generate consistent results for customers and cash flow.

Whether you're flipping sneakers, starting a vending route, or building a media brand—your system will determine your ceiling. Talent without systems burns out. Hustle without systems stagnates.

There are six core components you need to build into any system:

Input Source – Where opportunity or customers come from.
Operations Flow – How the work gets done and in what order.
Delivery Method – How the value gets to the end user or buyer.
Financial Controls – How the money is tracked, stored, reinvested, or protected.
Growth Loop – How you learn, improve, test, and grow.
Exit or Evolution Strategy – How this becomes scalable, sellable, or sustainable.

———

❌ MYTH VS. ✅ REALITY

❌ **MYTH:** "If you're good at what you do, the money will come."

✅ **REALITY:** Skill without systems will trap you.

This is how people get stuck as high-paid freelancers or solo entrepreneurs for 10+ years. They're exceptional at *doing the thing* but terrible at *building the machine that does the thing without them*. This is also how some of the most talented people in the world end up broke, stressed, and secretly resentful of the business they built.

Don't build a new job. Build a new machine. Systems are the secret. They don't just make you money—they give you back your time, your brain space, your peace.

———

📊 ACTION PLAN

Here's your step-by-step blueprint. Don't rush this. Circle back when you're stuck.

1. 👉 **Name Your Core Output**

Ask: *What does my system exist to deliver?*
Examples:
"Deliver cold bottled drinks to working-class customers in 10 neighborhoods."
"Flip sneakers for 2x ROI via IG and sneakerhead Discords."
"Provide editing services to indie authors in under 10 days."
If you don't know what the core output is, your system will become bloated or break under pressure. Write this clearly. Tape it to your wall if you need to.

2. 👉 **Map the Inputs and Intake**

Where does opportunity enter your world? Your system starts at the very first point of contact.
Examples:
Craigslist, OfferUp, or Facebook Marketplace (for product sourcing)
Instagram DMs, Etsy messages, your business email
Inbound leads from Google search or vendor referrals
You must systematize this. Whether through templated replies, intake forms, or automatic response sequences—you need a way to handle the front door.

3. 👉 **Define the Ops Flow**

What are the steps from intake to delivery? List them out. Don't overcomplicate. Just capture the actual sequence.
Example for a sneaker resale operation:
Source new drop info from sneaker forums.

Buy with bot or direct.
Photograph and list on IG + eBay.
Track messages, negotiate, close sale.
Pack and ship via standard 2-day box.
Record the sale in the spreadsheet.
Now ask: What can be templated? What can be automated? What can be outsourced? Systems are built from the answers to those three questions.

4. 👉 Secure the Delivery Path

Your delivery method should be consistent, reliable, and ideally *not dependent on your physical presence.*
Some examples:
Digital delivery (eBooks, templates, consulting links)
Reliable shipping systems (pre-labeled boxes, USPS pickups)
In-person but predictable (same route vending machines restocked every Sunday)
The more consistent the delivery method, the easier it is to maintain trust and cash flow.

5. 👉 Track the Money with a Simple System

A business that doesn't track its cash is not a business. It's a very stressful hobby.
Set up the following minimum:
A spreadsheet or accounting app (e.g., Wave, QuickBooks, Notion)
Categories: Revenue, Expenses, Reinvestment, Debt Paydown, Taxes
Weekly review: Check inflow, outflow, and ROI by product or service
Even if it's just $200 a month right now—you're training yourself to treat your money like a machine, not a mystery.

6. 👉 Create Your Feedback & Growth Loop

Ask after every cycle:
What worked?
What failed?

What's worth testing next?

Track these answers somewhere. Use that loop to tweak your process. This is how tiny systems become six-figure machines over time. You won't need a 10-person team to grow—you'll just improve the machine, quarter after quarter.

7. 👉 Document It All (So You Can Replace Yourself)

This is the secret to going from Light Blue (entrepreneurial job-owner) to Yellow (passive Gen 1 income).

Make a system manual. Could be a Google Doc. Could be a 5-minute Loom video. Could be Post-it notes on your mirror. But get it OUT OF YOUR HEAD and into a repeatable format.

Because until your system lives somewhere other than inside you... it isn't real. It isn't free.

8. 👉 Build an Evolution Path or Exit Plan

Every good system is designed to either:
Grow without you
Be handed off
Be sold
Ask:
"If I took 2 weeks off, what would break?"
"If I wanted to sell this system tomorrow, what would be missing?"
"What pieces can be modular—so I can upgrade or swap out later?"
Systems that can't evolve eventually suffocate. Build yours to expand or hand off.

🧭 WHY THIS MATTERS (AND WHERE IT FITS INTO THE BIGGER PLAN)

Flipping is the first freedom. But systems give you **sustained freedom**.

They don't just free up your schedule—they protect your energy, scale your money, and create something bigger than your next hustle.

Every time you build a new system, your earning power multiplies.

Every time you tighten a system, your stress decreases. Every time you document a system, your freedom expands.

Don't skip this chapter. Come back to it every time you level up. Because whether you're running vending machines, flipping thrift store finds, launching eBooks, or consulting on weekends...

You are a system builder now.

And system builders don't just make money.

They make machines that print it.

💥 READY FOR MORE?

A system without scale is like an engine that never leaves the driveway. You've done the design work—now it's time to grow. Because if it can't grow without you, it's not a business. It's a bottleneck.

———

📌 FOOTNOTES & CITATIONS:

Sources and citations for this chapter can be found in the back of the book under "Footnotes and Citations."

TWENTY-FIVE
NO SYSTEM, NO SCALE

Why Passive Income Needs a Machine—Not a Moment

 **CONCEPT:**

Passive income gets sold as a fantasy: do the work once, and the money just rolls in.

The reality is far less dreamy—and way more powerful.

Passive income is a system.

It's not a single product, or one lucky deal, or a viral success story.

It's a machine you build—brick by brick, process by process, hire by hire.

If you don't have a system, you don't have a shot at scaling.

And if you can't scale, you're not truly free.

This is the principle:

"Passive" doesn't mean silent. It means separated. You've built a system that earns even when you're not the one turning the crank.

———

🧠 THEORY:

In *The E-Myth Revisited*, Michael Gerber lays out something few entrepreneurs ever hear:

Most small business owners don't own businesses—they own jobs. And often, multiple jobs.[1]

The entrepreneur starts out as the technician: the person who makes the product, answers the phones, writes the content, drives the sales. You're the whole team.

But if you stay there—just doing all the work—you'll burn out.

That's not a system. That's a sweatbox.

The real goal? To build a business or asset that works without you.

That doesn't happen by accident. It happens when you stop working *in* the business and start working *on* the business.[1]

Even if your asset isn't a traditional business—say it's a rental property, a vending route, or a content site—the principle stays the same:

You need a system. Systems create structure. Structure creates scale.

A real estate investor has a system for screening tenants, setting rents, hiring repair teams.

A digital product creator has automations for delivery, email marketing, and customer support.

A flipper has suppliers, turnaround time rules, listing standards, and market analysis cycles.

What they all have in common is this: a system.

Without it, nothing's passive. Without it, nothing lasts.

———

❌ MYTH VS. ✅ REALITY

❌ **The Myth:** "Just make money while you sleep."

✅ **The Reality:** Until you've built a system, **you're** the system.

And when you're the system, you don't sleep—you grind.

That's why people who work overtime for someone else are still poor.

They're leveraging their time to power someone else's passive income machine.

That employer already made the system. You're just the fuel.

Flip it.

Build your own.

Structure it so the machine makes the money—not your minutes.

———

📊 ACTION PLAN

Here's how to turn a dream into a real income engine:

A.👉 Start as a Solo Generalist

In the beginning, you'll wear every hat. That's normal.

You'll be the tech guy, the marketer, the product builder, and the customer service rep.

But don't get stuck there.

Treat every task like a temporary position—because it is.

You're building the blueprint, not the prison.

B. 👉Reinvest Profits into Specialists

Once you get some income flowing, don't spend it—leverage it.

Reinvest into team-building. Systemize what you've learned.

Who you'll need (even part-time or freelance):

- Legal: lawyer to form entities, contracts, compliance
- Financial: accountant, bookkeeper, tax advisor
- Operations: assistant, logistics, scheduling, CRM support
- Marketing: social media, email sequences, copywriting
- Tech: website management, automation, analytics
- Advisors: mentor, business strategist, niche consultant

This doesn't have to be expensive at first—but it has to be intentional.

Every role you fill with a system or a person is one more brick in your path to freedom.

C. 👉 Build Around These 5 Core Functions

No matter your asset type (small business, rental, IP licensing, etc.), these pillars matter:

- **Lead Generation** – Who finds you and how?
- **Conversion** – How do they buy or commit?
- **Fulfillment** – How do they get the product/value?
- **Follow-up** – What keeps them coming back?
- **Support/Legal/Compliance** – What protects the machine?

Design those five steps like gears in a machine.
Each one needs to be testable, tweakable, and eventually delegatable.

———

🧭 WHY THIS MATTERS (AND WHERE IT FITS)

This chapter is the hinge of your wealth journey.

Up until now, we've talked about income streams, flips, and financial habits.

But this? **This is the turning point.**

Because no matter which lane you choose—digital products, consulting, real estate, flipping—**scale only happens through systems.**

Without a system, your income will always require your time.
And that's not freedom. That's just a fancy job.

But when you build a system...
When you begin to lead your income, not just earn it...
When you hire well, document well, automate smart, and protect what you've built...

That's when money shows up while you're on vacation.

That's when your asset keeps growing even when life gets busy. That's when you sleep—and your system still earns.

Success is a team sport.
You're the captain. Build your team. Build your system. Own your time.

———

💥 READY FOR MORE?

Scaling without a system is a recipe for burnout. But even with a system, many people make one critical mistake: they expect it to be passive from day one. They hear "passive income" and imagine money on autopilot—without realizing the build phase is anything but passive. Before you dream of sleeping through deposits, let's talk about what it really takes to earn that rest. See you in the next chapter.

———

📌 FOOTNOTES & CITATIONS:

Sources and citations for this chapter can be found in the back of the book under "Footnotes and Citations."

TWENTY-SIX
PASSIVE ISN'T PERFECT

What Most People Get Wrong About "Money While You Sleep"

💡 CONCEPT

Passive income is one of the most misunderstood financial goals. It's sold as the dream: "make money while you sleep." But nobody tells you how much work happens before the sleeping part.

Real passive income is a result, not a starting point.

Until it's a system, it's not passive.

––––

🧠 THEORY:

There's a reason passive income sits at the top of the wealth ladder—it takes leverage, patience, and execution. Most of what people call "passive" is actually leveraged or semi-passive, which means you work up front and get paid later... sometimes.

The real goal isn't just less work. It's better work: smarter, higher-yield, and longer-lasting.

Passive income means:

- You are not exchanging time for money anymore
- The income continues without constant involvement
- There is a system doing the heavy lifting

It does not mean:

- No maintenance
- No risk
- Instant results

———

❌ MYTH VS. ✅ REALITY

❌ **Myth:** Passive income is easy money with zero effort.

✅ **Reality:** Passive income is hard-earned automation. You either built the system or bought into one someone else built. Either way, it's earned freedom, not free money.

📊 ACTION PLAN: FROM WORKLOAD TO WORKFLOW

Let's break this down in stages so you don't get seduced by surface-level shortcuts.

1. 👉Choose the Right Passive Lane

There are **five major passive income lanes** (see *Colors of Money* for the deep dive), but here's the cheat sheet:

Lane	Description	Startup Cost	Time Involvement
Real Estate	Rental properties, land	High	Medium (at first)
Royalties	Books, music, software	Medium	High (front-loaded)
Digital Products	Courses, templates	Low to Medium	High (front-loaded)
Dividend Stocks	Income from shares	High	Low (ongoing research)
Business Ownership	Systems that run w/o you	High (or time)	High until systemized

Not all passive income is right for every season of your life. Choose your lane based on:
How much **capital** you can risk
How much **time** you can put in early
What kind of **system** you can build or buy into

2. 👉"Until It's a System, It's Not Passive"

You must build or plug into a **repeatable process**. No system = no scale.

This is where most people fail. They confuse a **one-time win** with a **working machine**.

That course you launched once? Not passive.
That house you just bought? Not passive.
That product you posted? Not passive.
Now if you:
Automate the marketing
Delegate the operations
Systematize the delivery
Then you've got something close to passive.

3. 👉Stop Romanticizing the Sleep Money

The phrase *"money while you sleep"* sounds sexy, but here's what nobody tells you:
You'll lose sleep **building** it.
You'll question your value when it flops.
You'll work harder upfront than any 9–5 could ever demand.

And when it finally works? It still needs **monitoring** and **maintenance**.

Here's the difference though:
That effort **compounds**, unlike a paycheck.

———

🧭 WHY THIS MATTERS (AND WHERE IT FITS INTO THE BIGGER PLAN)

The lie that passive income is instant sets people up to quit too soon.

The truth? Passive income is **earned peace**. Not immediate. Not magic. But worth it.

When you reframe passive income as a **future result** of systems, strategy, and sweat—you stop chasing unicorns and start building engines.

In the plan:

First you do flips →

Then you save and stack →

Then you test a lane →

Then you build the system →

Then (and only then)... it's passive.

———

💥 READY FOR MORE?

Passive income starts when you stop mistaking busyness for business. Labels don't create freedom—structures do. But too many people don't even know what game they're playing. Before you can win, you need to name your lane. Let's examine this in the next chapter.

———

📌 FOOTNOTES & CITATIONS:

———

Sources and citations for this chapter can be found in the back of the book under "Footnotes and Citations."

———

TWENTY-SEVEN

THE DIFFERENCE BETWEEN A JOB, A GIG, A HUSTLE, & A BUSINESS

Know the lanes, and remember The Colors of Money™

 **CONCEPT:**

You Can't Own What You Can't Name

There's a reason the language we use around money is so slippery.

"Side hustle."

"Entrepreneur."

"Boss babe."

"Self-employed."

"Freelancer."

"Business owner."

People toss these labels around like they're interchangeable. But they're not. And if you don't know what lane you're actually in, you won't know what rules to play by—or when it's time to level up.

Here's the truth:

Most people are in motion... but still renting their time.

That includes folks working full-time jobs *and* those running what they think are businesses. If you don't understand the difference between a job, a gig, a hustle, and a business, you can't evolve past your current tier.

Clarity is power. And this chapter gives you both.

———

🧠 THEORY:

The Ladder from Time-for-Money to Ownership

Wealth grows on a ladder. Every rung gives you more leverage—and more control.

Let's define the four major rungs clearly:

Job → You trade time for money under someone else's system.

Gig → You still trade time for money, but you choose your clients or hours.

Hustle → You're building something *you own*, but it still depends on your effort.

Business → You own a system that earns, even when you don't show up.

Each has its place. But only the top two move you toward real freedom.

The goal isn't to shame where you are—it's to **name it**, so you can grow with strategy.

Myth vs. Reality: "I Work for Myself" vs. "I Own a System"
The Myth: If You Work for Yourself, You Own a Business

A lot of people say "I'm a business owner," when they're really just self-employed or hustling.

Here's a hard truth:

If you stop working and the money stops, you don't own a business. You own a job.

Being self-employed is *not* the same as owning a business. You may have your own clients. You may be a 1099. You may invoice like a boss—but if you're still the engine, you haven't escaped the time-for-money trap.

The Reality: A Business Runs Without You

The real distinction is this:

A **gig** pays you for tasks.

A **hustle** pays you for effort you control.

A **business** pays you from **systems** and **assets**—not labor.

That system might be a laundromat, an online product, a team, or a service that runs with minimal input.

But it's the *leverage*, not the title, that defines it.

Owning a business means you've graduated from **rented effort** to **repeatable income**.

———

📊 ACTION PLAN:

Identify Where You Are—And How to Move Up

Here's a breakdown of each level, how to treat it, and what it takes to evolve upward:

1.👉 The Job: Stable but Capped

Definition: You trade time for a paycheck. You follow someone else's rules.

Examples: Teacher, nurse, cashier, corporate analyst, factory worker.

Pros:
Predictable income
Benefits (sometimes)
Clear responsibilities

Cons:
Limited control
Ceiling on earnings
No leverage or ownership

How to Treat It:
Use it to fund your real moves.
Don't confuse job security with life security.
Save aggressively and learn skills on the side.

How to Evolve:

Start a gig or flip alongside your job.

Invest in learning about income systems at TheColorOfMoney.com

2. 👉 The Gig: Flexible but Fragile

Definition: You offer services or labor on your terms—but you're still paid per task or hour.

Examples: Uber driver, tutor, freelance designer, TaskRabbit, Instacart, part-time contractor.

Pros:
You control your schedule
Quick money
Can stack multiple gigs

Cons:
No scalability
Burnout potential
Still trading time for dollars

How to Treat It:
Use gigs as cash flow, not a career plan.
Track every dollar—gig money disappears fast without structure.
Learn customer service, sales, and basic marketing—these skills will translate later.

How to Evolve:
Turn gig income into seed capital.
Start testing products or services you can scale or automate.

3. 👉 The Hustle: Control with Limits

Definition: You've started your own thing—maybe an online store, service, or creative brand—but it still depends on you.

Examples: Print-on-demand store, baking side business, Etsy shop, coaching, detailing cars, photography, personal training.

Pros:
You own it
You set the prices
You choose your clients

Cons:
If you stop working, the income stops
Still stuck in fulfillment
Prone to burnout or plateau

How to Treat It:
Respect your hustle as a real vehicle.
Document your processes.
Don't get caught chasing virality—instead, build repeatable routines.

How to Evolve:
Automate the repeatable parts (use tools, templates, systems)
Hire help—even part-time
Build infrastructure for scale (email lists, standard offers, evergreen products)

4. 👉The Business: Systems Over Sweat

Definition: You've created a system that earns income without requiring your daily involvement.

Examples:
Rental properties
Digital courses or memberships
Vending machines
Staff-run services (cleaning business, agency, repair team)
Licensing deals or IP royalties

Pros:
Time freedom
Asset ownership
Scalable income

Cons:
More setup risk and learning
Requires strong decision-making
Not always "passive"—you still lead strategically

How to Treat It:
Treat systems like gold. Build them, test them, and protect them.
Work *on* the business more than *in* the business.
Use income to buy time or expand intelligently—not to inflate your lifestyle too early.

How to Evolve:
Reinforce your systems (tech, team, templates)
Delegate strategically
Create new income layers that complement the first (stacked models)

————

WHY THIS MATTERS: YOU NEED A LADDER, NOT A LOOP

Too many people spend their lives on a loop:
Get a job
Pick up a gig to cover extra bills
Launch a hustle with no plan
Burn out
Go back to square one
Why?
Because no one taught them how to **think in levels.**
You can't jump from job to CEO overnight. But you *can* move from:
Job → Gig (cash flow)
Gig → Hustle (ownership)
Hustle → Business (freedom)
Each step has its lessons. But the goal is the same: **leverage over labor.**
The most dangerous trap isn't staying broke.
It's staying **busy**—but never building freedom.

Final Word: Name It So You Can Grow It

Language shapes reality.

If you think your gig is a business, you won't build the systems.

If you call your hustle a "company," but you're doing everything solo, you'll get stuck.

But when you name it right, you build it right.

Jobs fund you.

Gigs float you.

Hustles train you.

Businesses free you.

You don't have to feel ashamed of where you are.

But you *do* have to know what lane you're in—so you can climb out when it's time.

Because freedom isn't just about working for yourself.

It's about owning something that works *without* you.

And that starts with clarity.

———

💥 READY FOR MORE?

Once you know your lane, the next step is learning how to level up inside it. That starts with negotiation—not just for money, but for leverage. Because the people who win in business? They don't just talk. They listen. They ask. And they position. Let's examine this in the next chapter.

———

📌 FOOTNOTES & CITATIONS:

Sources and citations for this chapter can be found in the back of the book under "Footnotes and Citations."

TWENTY-EIGHT
LEARN TO NEGOTIATE ORANGES

Why Assuming Is Expensive and Asking Is a Superpower

💡 **CONCEPT:**

Most people negotiate with their mouth. The smart ones negotiate with their ears.

Whether you're flipping a product, brokering a deal, hiring a service provider, or trying to scale your business—negotiation is unavoidable. But most people only focus on what they want. That's like playing chess while staring at your own pieces. The real leverage is in understanding the other side's pieces—and more importantly, their motives.

School never taught us this. It trained us to argue, defend, and debate. Not to ask questions. Not to listen. Not to investigate someone else's true need.

And that oversight costs people millions.

———

🧠 THEORY:

Most failed negotiations don't fail because the parties can't agree. They fail because the parties don't understand what the other person actually values. And they never asked.

This is the key principle:

In a negotiation, spend 40% of your energy knowing what you want.

Spend 60% of your energy discovering what they want.

That second half is the power play. The treasure map. The leverage. The unlock.

I'm not asking you to be a people pleaser.

I'm asking you to become a problem solver.

Because when you solve real problems for people, money follows. Every time.

Myth, Then Reality:

Myth: The goal of negotiation is to get what you want.

Reality: The real win is when both parties walk away feeling like they got what they wanted.

Let me show you.

———

THE ALLEGORY:

"Jamie, Mario, and the Orange"

Let me tell you a story I want you to remember forever. It's deceptively simple. But it has made people better negotiators in one reading than most MBAs in five years.

Two people.

One orange.

A negotiation.

Jamie and Mario both want the same orange.

Jamie steps up first. She believes in fairness and efficiency. She offers what seems like a classic win-win:

"Let's split it down the middle—half and half."

Mario hesitates but agrees. Jamie carefully cuts the orange, measuring it down to the millimeter. She's proud of the clean, perfect halves. She hands one to Mario, keeps one for herself, and feels like she just crushed the deal.

Then something strange happens.

Jamie peels her half, tosses the peel in the trash, and savors the juicy fruit.

But Mario? Mario calmly peels his half, takes a plastic bag out of his backpack, and dumps the juicy fruit into a trash can—bagging only the peel.

Jamie gasps. "Wait—what the hell did you just do? You threw it away!"

Mario looks puzzled. "You did the same."

Jamie snaps, "I wanted the fruit!"

Mario nods. "And I only wanted the peel."

She stares at him, stunned. "Why didn't you tell me?!"

He looks back, quiet and calm:

"Why didn't you ask?"

And just like that—half the fruit she wanted is rotting in a trash bin, and Mario walks away with only half the peel he needed.

Both walked away feeling like they lost.

Breakdown:

If you read that story and thought, Why would anyone want just the peel?, then you missed the entire lesson.

It's not your job to judge what someone else values.

It's your job to find out what they value. And to never assume.

That's the beginning of real negotiation. The kind that wins. The kind that builds wealth, not frustration. The kind that builds allies, not silent enemies.

Whether you're buying a business, hiring a team member, or flipping a storage unit find—you need to start asking questions like:

"What's most important to you in this deal?"

"If we made this work, what would be the real win for you?"

"What do you absolutely need—and what's flexible?"

You'd be shocked how often people want something that costs you nothing to give them.

Sometimes they want faster delivery, or more trust, or a little public credit. Sometimes they want legacy, not money. Sometimes they want the peel, not the pulp.

If you don't ask—you'll never know. And that ignorance costs you the very leverage you were born to hold.

———

📊 ACTION PLAN:

Here's how to negotiate oranges—whether literal or metaphorical.

Step 1: Know what you actually want.

Not just the surface ask. What is your real goal? (Speed? Ownership? Residual income? Growth?)

Step 2: Ask about their peel.

Use open-ended questions early. This builds trust, uncovers invisible value, and often exposes a deal you never saw coming.

Step 3: Stop assuming people are like you.

This is where most negotiations go off the rails. You think, If I were them, I'd want...
No. You are not them. Ask. Listen. Confirm.

Step 4: Offer a trade, not a tug-of-war.

If you know what they really want, you can often offer it in a way that still protects or even enhances what you want. That's how people get deals nobody else can.

Step 5: Be okay with walking away.

If they're not willing to reveal their priorities, or if the terms don't align, walk. But now you walk with clarity—not assumption.

Why This Matters (and Where It Fits into the Bigger Plan):

This is deeper than sales or business.

Learning to negotiate oranges:

Makes you a more strategic thinker in every room.

Makes you emotionally intelligent without being manipulated.

Trains you to lead with curiosity, not control.

Helps you seize better deals, not just more deals.

Keeps you from wasting energy splitting the wrong parts of the damn fruit.

And more than anything—it reminds you that assumptions are expensive.

This chapter fits right in the middle of your wealth-building transformation, because it builds the bridge between knowing what you want and knowing how to get it without friction, waste, or regret.

School didn't teach you this. But life will charge you for not learning it.

Tattoo this chapter on your mindset:

Before you slice the orange, ask what they need.

That's where real wealth begins.

———

💥READY FOR MORE?

The best negotiators know this: you don't scale alone. At some point, you stop doing everything yourself and start building a team—strategically, not sentimentally. Let's break down who should be in your corner—and when to call them in. Let's examine this in the next chapter.

TWENTY-NINE
THE SUCCESS TEAM ROSTER

Wealth Isn't Solo—Here's Who You Need in Your Corner

💡 CONCEPT:

You don't build real wealth by yourself.

You may start alone, but you scale with support.

Wealthy people don't *just* leverage money.

They leverage *people*—legally, ethically, and smartly.

This is your **Success Team**: a curated circle of specialists who help protect, scale, and streamline your money systems.

Think of it like a sports team:

You're the captain. But every great team has a coach, a medic, a strategist, and support staff.

This isn't about hiring a bunch of employees right now.

It's about knowing *who you'll need, when you'll need them,* and *why they matter.*

———

🧠 THEORY:

You can't be your own everything forever. That's how you become over-worked, underpaid, and legally vulnerable.

Even solo businesses need structure.

Even creative hustles need tax protection.

Even successful flips need reinvestment strategies.

There's a point where doing it alone becomes *expensive*.

In time, knowledge, stress, and missed opportunities.

So instead of trying to learn everything…

Build your circle. Build your system.

———

📊 ACTION PLAN

Let each expert carry their part of the load—while you lead the vision.

The Core Success Team

Here's your starting five:

🛡 1. Lawyer

To help you form your LLC, write contracts, handle IP rights, and protect your backside legally.

📘 2. Accountant or Tax Strategist

To make sure your structure saves money, not just earns it.

They know where the legal deductions are. That's not a cheat—it's strategy.

📊 3. Bookkeeper

To keep your income and expenses organized. You don't need chaos. You need clean data.

🎯 4. Mentor or Business Coach

This is your sounding board. The one who sees your blind spots and helps you move smarter, faster.

💼 5. Banker or Funding Advisor

Relationships matter. When you're ready for capital (loans, lines of credit, funding), a *real* human who understands your goals makes all the difference.

Bonus Team Roles (As You Grow)

Tech Specialist – to set up automations, systems, website backends.

Marketing Support – for content, copy, email, ads, and visibility.

Virtual Assistant (VA) – for customer follow-ups, inbox management, scheduling, research.

Strategic Consultant – to help you plan your next scale move, acquisitions, or exit.

Insurance Advisor – to protect your income, liability, and assets.

Start small. Start smart. But start.

You don't need the whole team at once—but you *do* need a plan for how you'll build the bench.

———

🧭 WHY THIS MATTERS

Wealth is not random. It's built on relationships, routines, and reinforcement.

This chapter gives you the real blueprint wealthy people use. Now you have it too.

You can't outsource the dream—but you *can* build a team to protect it.

———

💥READY FOR MORE?

Once your system is moving and your team is aligned, the only thing left is fuel. This next part isn't about theory. It's about action. Capital flips. Smart leverage. Wealth in motion. You've built the machine—now it's time to fire it up.

———

📌 FOOTNOTES & CITATIONS:

Sources and citations for this chapter can be found in the back of the book under "Footnotes and Citations."

THIRTY

CHANGE YOUR LIFE

 **CONCEPT:**

Small change can change your life.

That's not just a motivational phrase—it's a blueprint. A principle. A mathematical truth.

You weren't taught this in school, but the corporations know it by heart. Why do you think so many fast-food chains, gas stations, and retail stores now ask, "Would you like to round up and donate your change?" They know what you weren't taught: **small change—when directed with precision and purpose—becomes big money.**

And not just "big money" in a vague sense. I mean capital—**money with direction, force, and reproductive power.** This book is packed with orange-seed ideas—small investments, small flips, small actions that can snowball into capital gain.

But even if you did nothing else except **redirect your current spending habits, collect your leftover change, and dedicate it to one focused mission—your capital gain account—you would begin to win.**

And win smartly.

————

🧠 THEORY:

Let's make this real.

You spend:

☕ $3.78 on a coffee

🥪 $5.13 on a sandwich

🛒 $9.91 on a last-minute online deal

Do you see it? The spare cents? The unnoticed slivers?

Now picture **all that change collected and put to work**. I don't mean buried in a jar. I mean **employed**. Put into small flips. Low-entry capital plays. Flipping a domain name. Reselling a limited sneaker drop. Running one tiny marketing test for your digital product.

That's the difference between **money being spent and money being flipped**.

Change may seem like the loose leftover, but in reality? It's often the only money you allow to slip away without guilt. That makes it dangerous when you're unfocused—but powerful when you are.

————

❌ MYTH VS. ✅ REALITY

❌ **Myth**: "It's just a few cents—it doesn't matter."

✅ **Reality**: Every penny counts when it's focused and intentional.

❌ **Myth**: "You need big money to invest."

✅ **Reality**: Small capital can fund flips and plant seeds for real growth.

❌ **Myth**: "Spare change is throwaway money."

✅ **Reality**: Spare change is stage-one capital—don't throw it away, deploy it.

————

📊 ACTION PLAN: THE FIVE-YEAR ORANGE FUND CHALLENGE

Here's your challenge, and it's a game-changer.

Commit to never spending a penny of change for the next five years.

Not the coins in your hand.

Not the round-up cents in your checking account.

Not the difference between budgeted and actual expenses.

Instead, all of it goes into a **designated capital fund**—a place for your flips, your first micro-investments, your asset entry plays. This is your **Orange Fund**: the capital you're cultivating specifically for growth.

You don't need a $10,000 windfall. You need daily discipline. Small deposits. Weekly reviews. And strict enforcement of a single rule: **This money doesn't get spent. It gets flipped.**

———

🧭 WHY IT MATTERS

Let's talk about impact.

Here are just a few examples that might only require a few dollars of seed capital:

Buy a domain name on sale and resell it.

Purchase and resell a trending limited-edition item.

Run a $20 ad for a digital product you created.

Print five copies of a short e-book or planner and test sales at a local shop.

Buy low-cost business cards to test your consulting pitch in your neighborhood.

These aren't dreams. **They're doable.**

They're small-box plays from the **"Small Bucks, Big Gains"** chapter. But you need the fuel to make them happen—and that fuel starts with your change.

Most people could save **hundreds or even thousands a year** in change—but only if they track it.

And the magic isn't in the math.

It's in the **focus.**

Money, like energy, follows focus. It compounds where it feels safe, seen, and directed. You don't need to believe in "money magic" or manifesting to understand that **structure and consistency turn almost anything fertile.**

Even your spare change.

One Last Thought: The Orange Fund Rule

Let's lock this in:

"Every penny of spare change you control shall be deployed for capital growth only—never spent, never leaked, never forgotten."

Give it its own account, envelope, jar, or app—whatever you need. But let this be sacred. Let this be your signal to yourself that you're changing direction. That you are **no longer a passive spender, but a deliberate builder.**

You're not too late. You're not too far behind.

You don't need a windfall.

You just need **frictionless discipline in one area**. Start with change.

Every journey toward freedom starts with a small redirect:

A pause.

A decision.

A new story.

Here's yours:

"I saw the game. I stopped throwing away the pieces. And I started playing to win."

That's how your life changes.

One penny at a time. On purpose

———

💥 READY FOR MORE?

When you start directing your loose change with purpose, something shifts. You stop waiting for "enough" to start—and start making moves with what you've got. Because once you see what small change can do, you're ready for the next test: what can $40 flipped do for your future? Let's examine it in the next chapter.

———

📌 FOOTNOTES & CITATIONS:

Sources and citations for this chapter can be found in the back of the book under "Footnotes and Citations."

THIRTY-ONE

SMALL BUCKS, BIG GAINS

Because You Don't Need a Lot to Get Started.
You Just Need to Start.

💡 CONCEPT:

Most people wait for a windfall before they think they can do something meaningful with money. But what if you could flip that belief on its head —and instead start with what's already in front of you? This chapter is about unlocking small capital gain moves that can transform your financial rhythm. It's not just about how much you make—it's about using movement, not just muscle. The first $40 you flip could teach you more about power than any paycheck ever did.

———

🧠 THEORY

We live in a system where capital is the game—and yet most people only play on one side: consumption. They buy. They borrow. They spend. But the other side of capitalism—**flipping, selling, creating, leveraging**—is where the power lies. This chapter plants your first flag on that side.

This is where you start to **train your capitalist muscles.**

You'll learn how to take **small capital gains**—profits earned through a one-time deal, flip, or creation—and use them to either:

🔼 / 🔽 **Flip Down**: Use the profit to pay off debt (without touching your paycheck).

🚀 **Flip Up**: Reinvest the profit into a passive income-producing asset.

This distinction is critical. If debt reduction is your emotional priority, flip down. If your debt is stable and you're ready to shift into income generation, flip up.

Either way—you're **reducing your reliance on earned income**. You're taking steps toward financial freedom, one flip at a time.

———

❌ MYTH VS. ✅ REALITY

❌ **MYTH**: "If I don't have a lot to start with, I can't do anything smart with money."

✅ **REALITY**: You don't need a lot—you need a shift in mindset. Capital gain doesn't only happen in boardrooms and brokerage accounts. It happens at yard sales, in the gig economy, at flea markets, online resale, or from skills you already have.

In fact, many people are already *spending* on things they don't need—coffee, subscriptions, clothes—without ever seeing that as risk. But a calculated $20 flip scares them.

Here's the shift: **When you know how to recover, the fear of loss shrinks.**

That $20 wasn't lost. It was tuition. You'll make it back next flip. And now you've learned.

———

📊 ACTION PLAN: *THE FLIP LIST (INTRO)*

We'll go deeper on these in a later chapter (**"The Flip List"**), but here's a preview of **doable, real-world flips**, starting from extremely low risk and moving into medium/higher:

① Ultra-Low Risk / Entry-Level
Sell unused household items on OfferUp, eBay, Craigslist, Mercari
Resell bulk candy/snacks at work or school
Print-on-demand t-shirts with a basic Canva design
Digital templates (resumes, invoices) on Etsy or Gumroad
Sell books you already own via BookScouter

② Low–Medium Risk / Skill-Builder Flips
Refurbish and resell furniture from Facebook Marketplace
Sell small freelance services (editing, design, voiceover)
Purchase & flip underpriced items from thrift stores
Buy and resell bulk goods on Amazon FBA or eBay
Flip used phones or electronics locally

③ Medium–High Risk / Capital Confidence Builders
Rent out a camera, drone, or car on peer-to-peer platforms
Buy a vending machine and place it at a local shop
Invest in a beginner website (domain + hosting) and flip it
Run a one-day workshop or online class for a skill you have
Buy low-competition inventory and flip it during high season
The key is to **start where you are, with what you have.**
You don't need to go big—you need to go **smart**.

———

WHY THIS MATTERS (AND WHERE IT FITS IN THE BIGGER PLAN)

This is the chapter that teaches you to **move**. It's where passive income stops being a dream and starts being a direction.

This is how you:

Build confidence in your own ability to generate profit.

Reduce emotional dependence on your 9-to-5.

Train yourself to take **measured risks with manageable upside.**

Because once you see money move *because of you*, not just *to you*?

Everything changes.

And once you've made your first flip—you'll see that the rules of the game were never written in stone. They were just written by people who didn't expect you to read them.

But now you are.

————

🔔 FINAL NOTE BEFORE WE MOVE ON

We'll explore **"The Flip List"** in its own chapter soon. There, we'll break down practical, step-by-step examples for flips across every income and risk level. This is your launchpad—not your limit.

And after your first flip?

Consider documenting your journey. Starting a blog. Making a tutorial. Teaching what you just learned. That's how one small flip becomes a new income stream.

Each one, teach one—and profit along the way

————

💥 READY FOR MORE?

That first $40 flip isn't just about proof of concept—it's a key. A small win that unlocks a much bigger game. Because once you realize how far a single flip can go, you're ready to open the chest most people never even find. The Flip List isn't just strategy—it's your personal goldmine. Hidden in plain sight. Full of overlooked chances to build, stack, and shift your entire financial trajectory. The next chapter alone is worth the entire cost of this book.

————

📌 FOOTNOTES & CITATIONS:

Sources and citations for this chapter can be found in the back of the book under "Footnotes and Citations."

THIRTY-TWO

THE FLIP LIST

How to Spot, Execute, and Reinvest Capital Gain Opportunities

💡 CONCEPT:

A "flip" is when you buy (or find) something for one price and resell it at a higher price, creating a **capital gain**. It's not your salary. It's not passive income. It's a flash of profit—money that should be treated as fuel for something bigger. Every flip, no matter how small, is a rep for your investment muscles.

__Mindset Check:__ You're not just hustling—you're practicing capitalism.

———

🧠 THEORY:

Flipping trains three crucial wealth skills:

Opportunity recognition (learning to see undervalued things)

Value creation (cleaning, bundling, branding, storytelling)

Discipline with profits (not spending the gains on fast lifestyle)

The point isn't just to make money. It's to master how to move money and eventually **flip up** into passive income.

———

❌ MYTH VS. ✅ REALITY

❌ **Myth:** Flipping is only for people with extra time or a truck.
✅ **Reality:** You can flip with zero dollars, no car, and no storage space—if you start where you are and keep the goal in sight.
Flipping is more about **resourcefulness** than resources.

———

📊 ACTION PLAN

1. 👉**Pick a Category to Test First**

Here's a no-nonsense starter list. These aren't side-hustles you scale into businesses—they're flips:

Clothes (thrift, clean, resell)
Shoes (rare drops, vintage, kid shoes in good condition)
Phones & tablets (repair, unlock, resell)
Textbooks or study guides
Electronics (chargers, cameras, Bluetooth items)
Furniture (curb pickup, clean & post)
Bicycles or scooters
Collectibles (cards, coins, retro items)
Event tickets (buy early, resell within guidelines)
Kid toys & baby gear (always in demand)
Kitchen appliances (blenders, rice cookers, coffee makers)

2. 👉**Flip It Fast—Then Track the Results**

Track:
How long it took
Where you found it
What you paid (or if it was free)
How much you made

What part was fun vs annoying
This isn't busywork. It's your training journal.

3. 👉 Use the Profit Like a Weapon

Per The Colors of Money™ system:
Orange money = capital gains
Use **80% to flip up** into passive income or **pay down debt**
Use 20% to pay taxes or stash for reinvestment
You are not allowed to spend the profit on brunch, kicks, or hair appointments. Flip money funds freedom. Not fun.
🌱 Why This Matters (and Where It Fits Into the Bigger Plan)
You won't get rich off one flip. But you will change your self-concept.
Every dollar you flip confirms:
"I can spot value. I can move capital. I am not trapped."
That realization is fuel. Flip money is your ladder to bigger things—real estate, royalties, dividend income, automated businesses. But first, prove to yourself that you can turn something small into something more.
And now...
🔄 **BONUS: Flip Lanes for Every Life Stage & Location**
Because hustle looks different depending on your age, environment, and skillset.

🧃 Kid & Teen Flips (Ages 10–18)

(Adult help may be required for payment setup.)
Candy bundles or snack packs (school/event-friendly)
Custom friendship bracelets
Recycled chargers and cables
Shoelace designs or sneaker patches
Gaming add-ons or character skins
Holiday gift wrapping services
🎯 *Lesson:* Learn markup, consistency, and customer interaction.

👴 Older Adults & Retirees (55+)

Antiques or estate item resales
Refurbished furniture (cleaned, painted, resold)
Vintage consulting (help others price old valuables)
Handmade crafts (quilts, crochet, woodworking)
Guided local tours or talks
Downsizing or cleanout sales
🎯 *Advantage:* Time flexibility + lived experience = trust + profit.

🏙 Urban Hustles (Small-Space Friendly)

Curb alert furniture flips
Lease transfer services (finder's fees)
Custom tote bags, pins, and tees
Quick tech help (battery swaps, phone resets)
Sneaker/streetwear limited drop resells
Restaurant menu edits or design help
🎯 *Use your city's density and fast pace to your advantage.*

🌾 Rural & Small-Town Flips

Farm box pickups & deliveries
Yard sale finds resold online
Lawn tool rentals or micro-repairs
Handmade signage for events
Scrap metal collection & resale
Storage unit cleanouts with split profit
🎯 *In smaller towns, trust travels faster than advertising.*

🔍 Niche Identity Flips *(Market with respect, not stereotype)*

Cultural jewelry or textile resell (authentic sourcing)
Translation or localization for small businesses
Haircare starter kits (bundled by hair texture or routine)
Faith-centered products (planners, merch, devotionals)
Event helpers for community groups or religious centers
🎯 *Your background may be your edge—if you treat it like a strength*

🔍 Example Expanded Sections for *The Flip List*:

Flip Categories

Retail arbitrage (Target clearance, Walmart rollbacks, etc.)
Digital flips (domain names, NFTs, digital courses, pre-made Canva templates)
Free-to-paid (Facebook Marketplace curb alerts → eBay or OfferUp)
Refurb and resell (used electronics, tools, bikes, furniture)
Event arbitrage (concert or festival tickets)
Vintage or rare item resale (clothing, collectibles, books)

🌐 Websites & Platforms

Product sourcing: Alibaba, Liquidation.com, Craigslist, OfferUp
Selling platforms: eBay, Poshmark, Mercari, Etsy, Amazon (FBA or FBM)
Local resale: Facebook Marketplace, Nextdoor, LetGo
Digital flips: Flippa (websites), Gumroad (digital goods), Ko-fi
Ticket/event flips: StubHub, SeatGeek

💼 Tools for Tracking & Automation

Google Lens (for fast product ID and pricing)
eBay sold item filter (to verify what actually sells)
Amazon Seller App (to check profit margin after fees)
Notion or Trello board for tracking flips & profits

💥 READY FOR MORE?

Every flip gives you two doors: flip down to eliminate bad debt or flip up to build bigger assets. Both paths lead forward—but the decision matters. Let's explore how to turn each capital gain into a freedom move, no matter your starting point. Let's examine this in the next chapter.

 FOOTNOTES & CITATIONS:

Sources and citations for this chapter can be found in the back of the book under "Footnotes and Citations."

THIRTY-THREE

FLIP UP OR FLIP DOWN

How to Turn Any Profit Into Progress—Without Touching Your Paycheck

💡 CONCEPT:

Every capital gain—no matter how small—gives you a choice:

Flip down: Use that profit to pay down consumer debt.

Flip up: Reinvest that gain into a bigger asset with the potential to generate passive income.

Either path builds your financial freedom. The key is that you're not using your paycheck. You're not sacrificing your rent money or your job stability to move forward. You're using the gains from small, smart flips—side money, hustle profits, low-risk capital gains—to start shifting your foundation.

This is how you reduce dependence on your salary without wrecking your life in the process.

———

🧠 THEORY:

If you're buried in debt, your number one priority might be relief.

If you're barely scraping by, your focus might be breathing room.

If you're stable but stuck, you might be ready to build income that pays even when you don't clock in.

The solution in all three cases? Flipping.

Flipping is the training ground. Small risk, short-term commitment, real reward. Each successful flip gives you a gain. And each gain gives you a decision:

Flip down: Use it to pay off high-interest debt faster, reclaim your monthly cash flow, and lower your financial pressure.

Flip up: Stack your wins and aim for a bigger move—a rental unit, a vending machine, a peer-lending investment, an asset with recurring cash flow.

Either way, you're building financial musculature:

Learning to analyze marketplaces
Getting familiar with risk and return
Practicing strategy instead of panic
Building skill, not just hustle
And all without putting your main income at risk.

———

❌ MYTH VS. ✅ REALITY

❌ **Myth**: "My job is safe. I'll just use my salary to pay things down."

✅ **Reality**: Your salary is an illusion of stability. You don't see the real books.

You don't know if your employer's drowning in debt.

You don't know if the company is floating payroll with credit.

You don't know if the next wave of downsizing already has your name on it.

And when it happens, it happens fast. No warning. No notice. Just a locked door and a vague email.

Using your paycheck to pay down debt might feel responsible, but it can trap you in dependence. It locks you into a job you may outgrow—or worse, one that's quietly dying.

By flipping down or flipping up with outside gains, you start making moves without chaining your future to your employer.

———

📊 ACTION PLAN

Step 1: 👉 Assess Your Position

Do you have high-interest debt that's weighing you down?

Or is your debt manageable and you're ready to focus on income growth?

Your strategy starts with the answer.

Step 2: 👉 Generate Your First Capital Gain

Pick a small flip with low risk:
Sell something you no longer need
Buy and resell a trending item
Offer a simple weekend service (washing, delivery, setup, etc.)
Your goal is a win. Fast. Clean. No loans. No stress.
(*For specific flip ideas by cost and risk level, see the chapter "Small Bucks, Big Gains."*)

Step 3: 👉 Decide—Flip Down or Flip Up

Flip Down: Take your gain and pay off debt. Every $200 gain that cancels a $35/month payment is like giving yourself a raise.

Flip Up: Take your gain and reinvest into something bigger. A flip that funds a passive income play starts breaking the salary chain.

Step 4: 👉 Repeat

This is not a one-time play. This is muscle-building.
Repeat the process.
Track your debt reduction or income growth.
Build confidence.
Build optionality.

Step 5: 👉 Why This Matters (and Where It Fits into the Bigger Plan)

This is where freedom starts.
You're not just flipping items—you're flipping leverage.
You're flipping your mindset.
You're flipping your financial DNA from earn-spend-repeat to flip-decide-build.
Every decision to flip up or down builds your future:
Flipping down builds security, control, and breathing room.
Flipping up builds income, options, and independence.
And most importantly—both start separating you from salary dependence.
Because whether you like it or not, we live in a capitalist system. You can fight it, or you can learn it. You can fear it, or you can flip it to your advantage.
Learn the rules. Build the habits. Strengthen the muscle.
Flip with strategy, not emotion.
And choose your direction with intention.

💥 READY FOR MORE?

Once the flips start working, the temptation grows—spend on a lifestyle, or stack with leverage. This is where many people slip: they confuse access with freedom. But credit isn't your reward—it's a tool. And how you use it will either accelerate your growth or undermine it. Let's examine this in the next chapter.

📌 FOOTNOTES & CITATIONS:

Sources and citations for this chapter can be found in the back of the book under "Footnotes and Citations."

THIRTY-FOUR

LEVERAGE VS. LIFESTYLE

 **CONCEPT:**

Credit is not your emergency fund. It's not your savings. It's not your solution to a tough month. Credit is a tool—nothing more—and the way you use it determines whether it builds wealth or poverty. Most people confuse access with assets. But real leverage doesn't come from buying a lifestyle—it comes from using credit to build cash-flowing, self-liquidating opportunities that actually earn.

———

THEORY:

Credit can create capital leverage, or it can create lifestyle debt. One leads to freedom. The other locks you into a cycle designed by banks to keep you obedient, overextended, and impressed by a score that serves them more than you.

The credit system rewards predictable behavior—not profitable behavior. If you don't understand this, you'll spend your life chasing credit approvals instead of assets. But if you do? You can flip the system to fund capital gain deals and investments that generate returns—without ever relying on credit for survival.

Use credit to multiply capital—not replace it.

———

❌ MYTH VS. ✅ REALITY

❌ **Myth:** "Credit is just a tool—if I use it responsibly, it helps my lifestyle."

🧨 **Truth:**

Most people use credit as a buffer for poor financial planning. They treat it like extra income. That's not responsibility—it's dependency. A high credit score doesn't mean you're good with money; it usually means you're obedient to lenders.

✅ **Reality**

- Credit card companies design the system to keep you in debt indefinitely.
- They train you to use credit as a stand-in for savings—and reward you for staying in debt with points and prestige.
- Consumer debt is normalized: cars, clothes, vacations, even furniture.
- The credit score reflects indebtedness, not wealth.
- Even personal homes—often called "assets"—are consumer purchases unless they cash-flow.

Want to break the cycle? Flip the script.

Use credit only for well-researched capital gain plays.

Prioritize deals with a short timeline, clear exit strategy, and self-liquidating debt (the deal pays for itself).

No emotional purchases. No "I deserve it" energy.

Cash-in-hand should always precede the charge.

🔴 **This is the perfect time to reiterate what I call Red Money.** Consumer credit is red money. That means it's a powerful tool for creating poverty. Never use credit for consumer goods. Never for emergencies. That's what White Money is for—savings. (See *The Colors of Money*™, Chapter 19 for a full breakdown.)[1]

———

◫ ACTION PLAN

1. ☞ Audit Your Debt:

Categorize all debt as consumer debt (Red Money) or capital-producing debt (Bronze Money). Be ruthless.

2. ☞ Close the Gap:

Stop using credit to fill budget holes. Cut lifestyle down to match your actual cash flow.

3. ☞ One-Card Strategy:

Use one card for strategic credit-building only. Spend within a pre-planned "cash envelope" amount and pay it in full at month's end.

4. ☞ Score with Strategy:

Build a high credit score not to show off, but to access strategic debt—like down payments on property flips, business purchases, or short-term stock plays.

5. ☞ Cash Before Credit:

Track how long you hold money before spending. Build that muscle. Leverage follows patience.

———

🧭 WHY THIS MATTERS (AND WHERE IT FITS IN THE BIGGER PLAN)

This chapter flips a major mindset—from survival-based borrowing to strategic leverage. It's the bridge between your internal money identity and your external money systems. Without this shift, you'll default to old habits—trading long-term wealth for short-term appearances.

Understanding leverage versus lifestyle sets the mental boundary that protects your future.

You're not building credit to flex—you're building assets.

And assets, acquired wisely, become freedom.

———

💥 READY FOR MORE?

Using credit right is one thing. But when you're holding real assets—especially real estate—the stakes go way up. Refinance can be a smart move... or a financial trap dressed like progress. Let's talk about when to pull the trigger—and when to leave the gun holstered. Let's examine this in the next chapter

———

📌 FOOTNOTES & CITATIONS:

Sources and citations for this chapter can be found in the back of the book under "Footnotes and Citations.

THIRTY-FIVE

WHEN REFINANCE MAKES
DOLLARS AND CENTS

Why using debt wisely can build your freedom—or bury it.

💡 **CONCEPT:**

Once you've acquired an asset—especially real estate—you may be tempted to use leverage to grow. And while it's not the worst financial move you can make, **refinancing your personal home to access capital is risky business**. This is a mid-level problem, but a high-stakes one. You're no longer broke, you've done some things right, but you're now at the crossroads of potential expansion—or collapse.

Why? Because **you are on the hook**.

But this is also where things get dangerous. This is the **mid-game, where one wrong move could cost everything you've built.**

And here's where the confusion begins: Just because you *can* refinance doesn't mean you *should*.

Let's be clear:

Refinancing your personal home—even for business purposes— means you are responsible for paying that debt back. Period.

Even if you plan to buy a rental. Even if you want to start a business. Even if you believe it will "pay for itself." You are still personally on the hook. And that means the freedom you're chasing is already compromised.

———

🧠 THEORY

Real wealth isn't about what you can borrow. It's about what pays you **without requiring you** to show up.

And that's where we enter the world of ◼ **Bronze Money**.

◼ **Bronze Money** is business credit. But it's not just a loan—it's **strategic, self-liquidating leverage.** Meaning:

You don't pay it back with your salary

The asset pays the loan (think: tenants, product sales, automated systems)

If structured properly, **you can scale without overexposure**

However, if that debt isn't **disciplined, backed by margin, and tied to actual income streams**, you're playing financial roulette.

What Most People Do

Let's talk about common (and dangerous) refinance habits:

🏠 **You pull $100K out of your home equity** to invest in a rental. The market shifts, rents drop, or the unit sits empty. Now you're paying two mortgages—and that second one doesn't feel so passive anymore.

📈 **You refinance to "start a business"** but you have no system, no offer, no timeline for break-even—just vibes and optimism. That's not an investment. That's a very expensive dream.

💳 **You refinance to pay off credit cards**, but never change the habits. The cards fill back up and now you're in twice the debt, just at a different rate.

Refinancing without structure is like strapping a jet engine to your car **without learning how to steer.** You might get ahead—for a second. But you're flying blind.

The Bronze Money Criteria

Bronze Money is not a hack. It's a tool for people who understand timing, risk, and cash flow.

Here's how to know if your refinance strategy qualifies:

✅ The loan-to-value (LTV) is **under 50%**

✅ The income to repay the loan comes from **others**, not your labor

✅ The debt is tied to a business, property, or asset—not your personal home

✅ You've modeled worst-case scenarios (vacancy, rate hikes, unexpected repairs) and can still breathe

✅ You're not chasing speed—you're building sustainability

If **any** of those are missing, it's not ▨ Bronze Money. It's just **Red Money wearing a disguise.**

⚠️ *Reminder: Red Money is the most dangerous form of money. It's debt you must service personally—with interest, stress, and urgency.*

———

📊 ACTION PLAN

When to Refinance—and When to Walk Away

A. Never refinance your personal home to "start something" unless:

The risk is minimal
The LTV is conservative (50% or lower)
You can withstand long periods with no cash flow
You have backup capital in case the asset doesn't perform

B. Only refinance when it creates cash flow—not just liquidity.

A pile of cash that's not earning? That's just borrowed pressure. The asset must pay the debt **and** leave a surplus.

C. Treat refinancing as a business loan, not a bailout.

If you're "hoping this works," you're not ready.

If you've done the math, modeled failure, and planned for tax implications? Now we're talking.

D. Only consider ■ Bronze Money if:

You have a strong asset with provable income

The debt helps you **scale something proven**

You're expanding a system, not gambling on a guess

Why This Matters

When you get to this stage of your financial life—when you've built something worth protecting—it's easy to think you need to move fast.

But this is the part where **precision matters more than speed**. You're not playing checkers anymore. You're playing chess.

■ Bronze Money is a powerful financial weapon—when used with discipline.

Used recklessly, it turns your dreams into liabilities.

And here's the truth most people never say:

It doesn't matter if the asset is "in someone else's name." If it fails, the fallout is yours.

Be smart. Be strategic. Don't just learn how to borrow. **Learn when to walk away.**

Because when refinance truly makes dollars and cents—it protects your future, not just funds your next move.

💥READY FOR MORE?

If you've built right—flipped smart, leveraged clean, and stayed liquid—you're getting close to something powerful: escape velocity. The point where your momentum breaks gravity. But freedom isn't just about a breakthrough—it's about not falling back. Let's make it permanent see you in the next chapter.

———

📌 FOOTNOTES & CITATIONS:

Sources and citations for this chapter can be found in the back of the book under "Footnotes and Citations.

THIRTY-SIX
ESCAPE VELOCITY 🚀

Breaking Free from Financial Gravity

💡 CONCEPT:

Escape velocity is the speed an object needs to break free from the pull of gravity. In money terms? It's the sustained energy—mental, emotional, and strategic—you need to *break out of paycheck orbit*. Not touch the stars for a minute, not take a joyride, but *stay gone*.

This chapter is about how to **break free, stay free**, and fly.

If it feels hard, it was meant to be.

Breaking free financially is the same as leaving Earth's atmosphere— you don't coast into it. You blast into it.

———

THEORY

In space, gravity is constant. In life, so is **financial gravity**:

rent

debt

guilt

"what would people think"
keeping up appearances
old money patterns
systems you didn't create but still depend on
And like gravity, none of it asks your permission.
You don't leave that orbit with a raise or a bonus. You leave it with:

Mindset → motivation that's bigger than your pain
Momentum → action so consistent it becomes inevitable
Systems → automatic patterns that hold the line while you sleep

*Escape velocity is less about speed and more about **sustained thrust in a focused direction**.*
That's what gives you lift.
So here's the sequence:

Crawl: Learn to see the matrix—understand the money game you were born into.
Walk: Start simple. Budget. Save. Say no. Pick up financial vocabulary.
Run: Build habits. Flip. Sell. Learn leverage. Take smart risk.
Maximize: Improve systems. Automate. Free up time.
Fly: Income now outruns bills. You're floating. Still vulnerable—but moving.
Orbit: Systems run. Stress down. Identity changes. *You are no longer who you were.*

The problem? Most people are trying to **fly** when they've never even crawled. Or they keep stopping halfway up the arc—and crash back into the same job, same bills, same grind.

———

❌ MYTH VS. ✅ REALITY

❌ *Myth: "If it's hard, I must be doing it wrong."*
✅ *Reality: If it's easy, you're probably still on Earth.*

No one breaks free without resistance. Escape isn't gentle—it's violent. It rattles. It burns fuel. It requires sacrifice. It may even look reckless to people who've never left the launchpad.

People say, "You're working too hard," when you're trying to build momentum.

They ask, "What if it doesn't work?"

The better question is, "What if staying *here* is the biggest risk of all?"

The truth is:

You don't reach orbit in comfort.

You don't build velocity by waiting for the perfect time.

You launch, adjust in flight, and stay consistent *until the pull weakens.*

———

📊 ACTION PLAN

Step 1: 👉 Assess your current stage.

Ask yourself honestly:

Am I crawling, walking, or flying?

Do I understand *how* money flows, or am I just reacting to bills?

Do I have a system that protects me when I sleep?

Step 2: 👉 Build your launch pad.

You need fuel (money coming in), structure (where it goes), and fire (why you're doing this).

Build:

Emergency savings (fuel)

Debt control (fuel leaks)

A system for income + action + automation (launch plan)

Step 3: 👉 Set your sights on orbit.

This means *consistency without burnout.*

Automate payments and income streams where possible.

Reinforce productive habits weekly (check-ins, calendar blocks, monthly audits).

Stay aware of distractions that pull you back into gravity: toxic people, unnecessary spending, ego traps, comfort zones.

Step 4: 👉 Don't stop at the clouds.

When money starts coming in faster than bills, most people relax. *That's when gravity sneaks back in.*

If you're still required to clock in, or still stuck in the same cycle— *you're not in orbit yet.*

Keep the pressure on until:

Passive income is consistent

Debt is gone or minimal

Your systems run even on your worst day

Then? You fine-tune, not rebuild.

———

🧭 WHY THIS MATTERS (AND WHERE IT FITS INTO THE BIGGER PLAN)

This chapter is your turning point.

This is where you realize the money game isn't about income—it's about **velocity and freedom**. You can make six figures and still be stuck in gravity. You can live small and get free faster than your ego says you should.

Here's the truth no one wants to admit:

You will have to work *harder* at the beginning.

You will feel *heavier, tired, alone.*

Because gravity doesn't let go without a fight.

But if you keep your systems clean and your vision clear, you won't need to fight forever.

Eventually, the momentum starts carrying *you.*

Eventually, you're not looking at the sky.

You're in it.

———

💥 READY FOR MORE?

Once you break orbit, a funny thing happens: you start seeing opportunity everywhere. Not just once-in-a-lifetime shots—but constant, compounding chances to grow. But here's the thing—those chances have always been there. Now you're finally in position to answer the door. Let's examine this in the next chapter.

———

📌 FOOTNOTES & CITATIONS:

Sources and citations for this chapter can be found in the back of the book under "Footnotes and Citations.

THIRTY-SEVEN
OPPORTUNITY KNOCKS AGAIN (AND AGAIN)

Why "once-in-a-lifetime" is a myth and how to get ready for your next shot.

💡 **CONCEPT:**

Opportunity doesn't knock once. It knocks constantly.

But if you're broke, blind, or bound up in the wrong mindset, you won't hear it. And even if you hear it, you won't be ready to open the damn door.

This is one of the most dangerous lies society—and school—ever sold us:

"Opportunity only knocks once."

That myth turns failure into shame. It keeps you stuck, thinking your window has closed when in truth, your whole house is surrounded by doors.

The truth?

Opportunities are everywhere.

But the ones you're able to seize are directly proportional to how well you've prepared your finances, your mindset, and your money color game.[1]

🧠 THEORY:

Let's reframe.

Opportunity doesn't come around once in a lifetime.

It comes around constantly—in patterns, in seasons, in disguises. But you only see what you're trained to recognize. You only move on what you're resourced to pursue.

It's not the lack of opportunities keeping people broke.

It's the lack of preparation.

They saw the property... but didn't have the down payment.

They met the investor... but had no business plan.

They got the tip... but their credit was wrecked.

They got the call... but their schedule, job, or anxiety locked them down.

They weren't ready.

So the opportunity didn't pass them by.

They passed by the opportunity.

❌ MYTH VS. ✅ REALITY

❌ **MYTH:** "You missed your shot. It's over."

✅ **REALITY:** If you saw the opportunity, you'll see it again. But will you be ready next time?

That regret you feel when you miss out on a deal, a connection, or a turning point—it's not failure.

It's **signal**. It's life showing you what you care about. It's life handing you a **syllabus** for your next season.

Most people treat the opportunity they missed like a **funeral**.

You should treat it like a **checklist**.

Let it burn for a moment. Then turn it into a blueprint.

What did it require?

What were you missing?

What would it take to be ready next time?

Opportunity is a mirror. It shows you who you need to become. Not to chase the past. But to catch the future.

———

📊 ACTION PLAN

This chapter is not about mourning missed chances.

It's about **building readiness**—financial, emotional, and structural—for the next ones.

1. 👉 Write the One That Got Away

- Write down a missed opportunity that haunts or frustrates you.
- Don't glorify it. Just list the facts.
- Then list what it would've taken to say yes.
- Was it $10K down? Better credit? A month of prep?
- → **There's your training plan.**

2. 👉 Create Your "Yes Kit"

Start building what you need to say **YES** next time.

- Emergency cash or down payment stash? Build it.
- Clear calendar and time margin? Guard it.
- Network or team member? Find them now.
- Basic LLC, EIN, or presentation? Have it ready.
- → Most "lost" deals are lost due to hesitation, not ability.

3. 👉 Name the Opportunity Type (and Color)

Give that missed opportunity a color:

- 🟠 Orange = The perfect passive income play you weren't ready for.

- 🟢 Green = Long-range generational asset that could've paid you forever.
- ⚫ Black = One-time windfall you blew or froze on.
- 🔵 Blue – After paying bills & no other source of income, no money to invest.
- 🔴 Red = You faked the funds with debt and now you're bleeding.
- 🟡 Yellow = You understood it... but didn't have your first-level passive income setup.

Now track opportunities by color. Build readiness by hue.

4. 👉 Flip the Language

Stop saying:
"I missed my chance."
Start saying:
"I saw what I'm being trained for."
"I know what to be ready for next time."
You're not a failure.
You're in rehearsal.
The next show starts soon.

5. 👉 Fund from the Right Source

Advanced: When the next Orange (ideal) opportunity appears—**don't fund it with Blue (labor) or Red (debt).** Use Teal or White surplus money only.

Orange opportunities funded with Red debt become Orange regrets.

———

🧭 WHY THIS MATTERS (AND WHERE IT FITS IN THE BIGGER PLAN):

This is the money chapter for people who have felt the sting.
The ones who said, "If I just had the money..."
"If I just had known sooner..."

"If I just had one more shot…"

You do. You will.

But this time, you'll be ready.

Because now you know:

School didn't teach you to expect opportunity.

It trained you to fear missing out, but not to prepare for what's coming.

Let this book, this system, flip that for you.

You're building readiness. You're building a **"yes reflex."**

You're conditioning your money to move with purpose, precision, and patience.

And when Orange knocks again?

You're gonna open the door in full confidence and say:

"You're right on time."

———

💥 READY FOR MORE?

The people who win don't wait for perfect timing—they recognize patterns and move fast. But speed gets a bad rep. This next chapter clears it up: fast isn't fake. It's focused. And if you've built right, it's your strategy now.

———

📌 FOOTNOTES & CITATIONS:

———

1. The Colors of Money™. Developed by the author, Robyn La'More, is a proprietary financial framework that categorizes income types by risk, leverage, and wealth-building potential. Explanation in Chapter 19 School Didn't Teach You This. The Colors of Money™ Robyn La'More. All rights reserved.

———

THIRTY-EIGHT

THE FAST LANE ISN'T THE SCAM—IT'S THE STRATEGY

This chapter isn't about get-rich-quick. It's about get-free-on-purpose.

💡 **CONCEPT:**

You've Been Taught to Distrust Speed

When people talk about building wealth in 5 to 10 years, it raises eyebrows.

It *should*. You've been warned your whole life that "fast" equals "fake." That anything outside the slow-and-steady path must be a scam. Maybe you've thought:

If it sounds too good to be true, it probably is.

Wealth takes decades. That's just how it works.

Anybody promising freedom in a few years is probably trying to sell me something.

But what if speed isn't the scam?

What if slowness is?

What if the biggest lie you were ever sold in school and in life was that the only way to succeed financially is to work 40 years, follow all the rules, and *maybe* retire with enough?

This chapter isn't about get-rich-quick. It's about **get-free-on-purpose.**

There's a difference. And it's everything.

———

 **THEORY**

Systems Beat Time—Every Time

Speed doesn't come from magic. It comes from **systems.**

There are two kinds of financial growth:

Linear growth: You trade time for money. You save. You invest. You wait.

Accelerated growth: You build systems. You generate capital gains. You acquire cash-flowing assets. You reclaim control of time.

Linear growth depends on a long timeline.

Accelerated growth depends on **leverage and learning curves**.

The real reason most people stay broke for decades isn't because it takes that long to get rich. It's because they never build systems that generate income *without their labor*.

So they're stuck on the same treadmill, for years.

Fast-lane thinkers exit the treadmill and build their own path.

That path isn't effortless. It's not passive in the beginning. But it's **strategic**. And strategy is what gets you free.

———

❌ MYTH VS. ✅ REALITY

"Fast Means Risky" vs. "Fast Means Focused"

❌ **The Myth: Fast money = shady money**

You've seen it before: the guy with the rented Lamborghini, promising $100K in 90 days. The social media guru selling dreams, not plans. That's not a strategy. That's bait.

So it's no surprise that when someone says "You could build real wealth in 5–10 years," you brace yourself for the pitch. We've been conditioned to see *speed* as suspect.

But here's the truth:

✅ **The Reality: Fast isn't risky—it's just intentional**

Speed becomes possible when you:
Cut out distractions
Master a few high-leverage skills
Use capital flips instead of just salary
Stack assets in a precise order
Reinforce each win with discipline, not delusion
The people who get financially free in 5–10 years *aren't lucky*. They're intentional. They're strategic. And they **respect money enough not to waste a decade doing it the hard way**.
This isn't about shortcuts.
It's about **sequence, strategy, and scale.**

———

📊 ACTION PLAN

How to Strategize for the Fast Lane
You don't have to sprint. But if you want to be off the treadmill within 10 years, you need to move with intention.
Here's the five-stage game plan used by people who build wealth faster than the system ever taught you to believe:

1. 👉 Fix Your Foundation (0–6 Months)

Before you grow, you need to hold what you've got.
Build a $1K–$2K emergency fund
Cut unnecessary spending leaks
Set weekly money check-ins
Clear red money (bad debt) using capital flips
Remember: *Savings protect investments. Control comes before growth.*

2. 👉 Flip Small, Flip Fast (6–18 Months)

Start flipping for capital gains using low-risk deals. Learn the game: buy smart, sell fast, reinvest.
Sell used items for profit
Resell appliances, furniture, clothes, or tech

Offer freelance services with no-cost startup
Use 100% of this money to kill debt or seed next-level moves
This isn't side hustle fluff—it's your training ground for bigger gains.

3. 👉 Plant Your First Passive Seeds (18–36 Months)

Now you're ready to buy your time back piece by piece.
Invest in a vending machine, digital product, eBook, or ATM
Start earning $50–$300/month without working for it
Reinvest every dollar into growth—not lifestyle
*Passive income at this stage isn't about luxury. It's about **traction**.*

4. 👉 Scale or Stack (3–6 Years)

At this point, you choose your lane:
Scale a small business: Turn your flips or service into a system
Stack more passive income: Use capital to buy assets (real estate, licensing, royalties, dividend stocks)
Either route creates **income you don't have to work for daily**.
And both require skill—not luck.

5. 👉 Exit the Treadmill (6–10 Years)

Your monthly expenses are now covered by systems, not your salary.
That's not retirement. That's **freedom.**
You can keep working, but now it's optional.
You can chase big plays, but you're not desperate.
You can help others, expand, or disappear—because you own your time.
You didn't skip steps. You just stopped wasting time.

🧭 WHY THIS MATTERS: YOU CAN'T AFFORD THE SLOW ROUTE

The slow path doesn't just waste time. It **costs power**.

When you buy into the idea that wealth takes 40 years, you give up too much:

You delay your freedom.

You tie your future to someone else's pension or plan.

You settle for "one day" while inflation, burnout, and regret compound.

But when you realize speed is possible—you move differently.

You ask better questions.

You stop tolerating bad debt.

You stop waiting for permission.

You focus.

You stack.

You build.

————

📚 REAL CASE STUDY: MEET JAMIE

Jamie was 33, a single parent, working full-time with $5K in credit card debt and no savings. For years, she'd been trying to max her 401(k) but still living paycheck to paycheck.

When she found out about the 5–10 year strategy, she made three bold shifts:

Paused retirement contributions for 12 months to build control.

Started flipping clearance electronics online—averaged $400/month profit.

Used those profits to pay off debt in 8 months, then launched a small print-on-demand shop.

By Year 3, she had a $4,000 emergency fund, no debt, $600/month passive income, and had resumed retirement investing *with breathing room*.

Her total income didn't double—but her *freedom* did.

And she's now on pace to be work-optional by 40.

————

 FINAL WORD: FAST IS A STRATEGY, NOT A SCAM

You don't have to get rich tomorrow.

But you also don't have to wait 40 years.

When done right, *fast* doesn't mean fake. It means:

Focused

Adaptive

Strategic

Trained

So don't apologize for wanting your freedom sooner.

Just make sure you earn it on purpose.

This isn't about cheating the game.

It's about **changing the game** you were never meant to win.

And now?

You've got the map.

———

 READY FOR MORE?

The fastest way to internalize what you've built? Teach it. Not in a classroom—but in conversations, content, or mentorship. Because when you explain how you broke free, you deepen your own mastery—and strengthen your momentum. Let's explore this phenomenon in the next chapter.

———

 FOOTNOTES & CITATIONS:

———

No citations required. All examples and case studies are original.

———

THIRTY-NINE
TEACHING WILL HELP YOU LEARN

Real transformation comes when you teach

 CONCEPT: TEACHING MAKES YOU STRONGER

People think the goal is just to learn wealth principles—but real transformation comes when you teach them.

You don't need a degree. You don't need a massive audience. You just need to be a step ahead and willing to speak. Because when you teach, something powerful happens: you internalize. You stop skimming ideas and start breaking them down. You apply them more deeply. You revisit them with fresh urgency.

That's not just helpful—it's critical.

———

THEORY:

Teaching Creates Accountability, Insight, and Legacy

Some of the most powerful money lessons you'll ever encounter don't fully click until you say them out loud. Or until someone you care about looks back at you and asks, *"But how do I start?"*

You'll learn more from trying to explain a simple wealth concept to a teenager or friend than you might from reading three more books.

Here's why:

Accountability: When others are watching, you show up differently.

Insight: Questions from others surface gaps in your own understanding.

Legacy: You're building more than a bank account—you're building a tribe that thinks differently.

Even when you're still in process, teaching as you go roots your learning deeper. It also forces you to live it—especially when you're tempted to drift.

This book? It exists because I started teaching. The moment I committed to helping others understand wealth, I had to rise to the challenge of practicing what I preached. That alone changed everything.

❌ MYTH VS. ✅ REALITY

❌ **Myth:** *"I'll teach this once I've mastered it."*

✅ **Reality:** *You master it by teaching it.*

People wait until they've built the perfect system, hit every milestone, or feel fully confident before they open their mouth. That's not how growth works.

If you've read three chapters, you know more than the version of you who hadn't. That means you already have something valuable to pass on. Don't gatekeep your own growth.

Let's get one thing clear: teaching isn't about being perfect. It's about being *present* and *willing*.

🌱 Here's the truth:

You don't need to be rich to teach people about margin.

You don't need passive income yet to explain the goal.

You don't need to be debt-free to help someone understand how credit *isn't* money.

You only need *one step more clarity* than the person you're teaching. That's it.

———

📊 ACTION PLAN

How to Teach What You're Learning

You don't need a whiteboard or classroom. Start small. Go personal. Here's how to do it:

A.👉 Start With Your Circle

Pick 1–3 people you care about who might benefit from what you've learned. Then:

Share a single concept that resonated with you.

Ask them how they've experienced it.

Invite them to read a chapter of this book, or walk through a section with you.

Be honest about where *you're* still learning. Vulnerability builds trust.

B. 👉 Use Questions, Not Sermons

Instead of preaching, try:

"What do you think of this idea?"

"How do you handle your paycheck breakdown?"

"Have you ever thought about your money in colors?"

Let conversation lead.

C.👉 Lead by Example

Show what you're doing:

Share your margin goals or flips.

Celebrate small wins (e.g., "I used my change fund this month!")

Talk about where your money is going—and why.

Your actions teach louder than your lectures.

D. 👉 Document Your Journey

Even if no one sees it yet, write down:

What you're testing
What's working
What's still foggy
What you want to understand next
That becomes a manual for someone else—and a memory anchor for you.

E. 👉 Teach Your Kids Early (Or Re-Teach Yourself)

If you have children, start there. Simplify:
"Red money is debt money. We don't spend it on fast food."
"We save orange money for flips."
"We earn blue money from work—and we use it wisely."
Don't underestimate how much they're absorbing from your choices.

————

🧭 WHY THIS MATTERS: YOUR CIRCLE IS WAITING ON YOU

You are the key to someone else's financial awakening. And they're not waiting for a guru. They're watching you.

Every time you teach, even casually, you reinforce your own discipline. And when life gets hard—and it *will*—the people you've shared your journey with will remind you why you started.

Teaching builds infrastructure. It creates community. It reminds you that you're not just doing this for yourself—you're doing it for everyone who depends on you and for everyone who doesn't know where to begin.

And it's okay to be learning and leading at the same time.
You're not behind.
You're just getting started.

————

💥 READY FOR MORE?

Teaching locks in your growth—but it also sparks a new question: What now? Where do I go from here? If you've made it this far, you're not just informed—you're armed. And the next chapter? It's not a conclusion. It's ignition.

———

📌 FOOTNOTES & CITATIONS:

Sources and citations for this chapter can be found in the back of the book under "Footnotes and Citations.""

FORTY

WHERE FROM HERE?

 **CONCEPT:**

This is the beginning, not the end.

You've just finished reading the *real* rules of money—not the sanitized textbook versions, not the hype, not the hustle myths. These are the tools school never gave you. But the real question isn't what you've read—it's what you'll do with it.

Reading alone doesn't build wealth.
Action does.
Let's recap. Let's make a plan. Let's move.

———

THEORY:

You now know what most people never learn:

Money is a **tool**, not a trophy.

Not all income is equal—**money has colors**, and each color behaves differently.

Seeds (capital gain) and **Fruit** (passive income) matter more than hustle checks.

Savings isn't cowardice. It's **protection**.

Capital gains don't require miracles—just flips.

Spare change is startup capital if you direct it.

Passive income is **earned**—and rarely passive in the beginning.

School taught you to spend and pray. This teaches you to **plant and prosper**.

Different game.

Different outcome.

———

❌ MYTH VS. ✅ REALITY

❌ **Myth**: "This was a good read—time to go back to life."

✅ **Reality**: This is the *starting line*, not the finish. Apply it or lose it.

❌ **Myth**: "I'll wait until I have more money to invest."

✅ **Reality**: What you do with **small money** determines if you ever have big money.

❌ **Myth**: "I don't need to track my income sources."

✅ **Reality**: If you don't know your money's *color*, you can't shift your financial future.

———

📊 ACTION PLAN

A. 👉 Set Up Your Orange Fund

Create a separate bank account, envelope, or digital tracker.

Funnel **spare change, round-up money, and budget leftovers** into it.

Do not spend it. This is your capital gains engine.

B. 👉 Make One Flip This Month

Sell something.

Offer a micro-service.

Test a product.
Print and pitch a small booklet.
Prove your money can move.

C. 👉 Build Two-Tier Savings

Tier One: $1,000 emergency fund.
Tier Two: $500 car / $500 life cushion.
Your safety net protects your momentum.

D. 👉 Track Your Money Color Weekly

At week's end, label your dollars:
⚫ **Gray** = Spent non-productively
🟠 **Orange** = Capital Gains
🟢 **Green** = Passive
Goal: Turn Gray → Orange → Green.
Result: Progress without burnout.

———

🧭 WHY IT MATTERS

This isn't theory anymore.
It's a system you can build on for life.
The next book—*The Colors of Money™*—dives deeper:
What each color represents
How to **recognize** it in your life
How to **transition** toward leveraged income
How to build a **money system** that protects and scales
You're not just learning how to earn.
You're learning how to own. How to flip. How to lead.
Your income isn't the goal. **Your income structure is.**

———

🏁 ONE LAST THOUGHT

You've read enough books.

You've made enough excuses.

Now it's time to build something real.

If this book sparked a new language—**use it**.

If it reminded you of old power—**wield it**.

If it stirred something inside—**trust it**.

Your past doesn't define your wealth.

Your patterns do.

Start the shift.

Keep your Orange Fund sacred.

Plant every flip with purpose.

Track your colors.

Protect your white.

Grow your green.

One change. One flip. One rule you keep.

School didn't teach you the rules.

But I just did!

You now know what school didn't teach you.

This isn't the end—it's your launch point.

GLOSSARY

The Colors of Money™[1]

Red Money — Debt Money

Money you don't actually have—borrowed money from credit cards, loans, or financing. Red Money comes with strings attached: interest, risk, and often regret. It's the riskiest money of all and should be used with caution, if at all.

Red Money isn't "real" money—it's a debt instrument.

Blue Money — Salary Money

Income earned through direct labor, usually in the form of hourly wages or salaries. This is the most common and most taxed form of income. You trade your time for money, and when you stop working, the money stops too.

Teal Money — Entrepreneurial Money

Income earned from ownership-based work. You control the operation, but you're still actively involved. Teal Money bridges labor and leverage. You own the business—but the business still owns your time.

Orange Money — Capital Gains

Money made when you buy low and sell high—flips, stock trades, real estate sales, side hustles, and other growth-based profits. It's strategic, often active, and carries risk—but it can also build wealth quickly when used wisely.

Black Money — Windfalls & Wildcards

Unpredictable, often untaxed, sometimes risky money. This includes lottery winnings, gifts, lawsuit settlements, or anything you didn't plan for. It can be a blessing—or a curse— depending on how it's handled.

Yellow Money — Passive Income (Generation 1)

The first level of passive income. This includes royalties, rental income, licensing fees, and other income streams that keep flowing without constant labor. The key: build it once, benefit many times.

Green Money — Passive Income (Generation 2)

Money earned by reinvesting your Yellow Money into additional passive streams. This is next-level freedom—money that grows itself. Green Money is how you shift from working smart to wealth that works for you.

[1] *All Color-based terms are part of* The Colors of Money™ *system, a proprietary framework created by the author, Ms. Robyn La'More. Trademark Pending Colors of Money LLC*

Glossary Terms Contuined:

Assets

Anything you own that has value and can be converted into cash. Assets include real estate, cash, stocks, businesses, intellectual property, and anything that contributes to your net worth.

Compound Interest
Interest calculated on both the original amount of money (the principal) and the interest already earned. This is how money grows faster over time.

Depreciation
The reduction in value of an asset over time, often due to wear and tear or market changes. Cars and electronics are common examples.

Emergency Fund
Money set aside to cover unexpected expenses or financial emergencies. A safety cushion—not an investment.

Escape Velocity
The point at which your income from assets or systems exceeds your basic living expenses—allowing you to break free from paycheck dependence.

Flip / Flipping
Buying something at a low price and selling it at a higher one to make a profit. Can apply to real estate, products, websites, or services.

Liquidity
How quickly and easily something can be converted into cash without losing value. Savings are highly liquid. Real estate is not.

Net Income
Your actual take-home pay after taxes, expenses, and deductions. Net income is what you keep, not just what you earn.

Ownership
Having control and financial rights over an asset, company, or income stream. Ownership builds leverage and freedom.

Pay Yourself First
A strategy where you put money into savings or investments before spending on anything else. It prioritizes your future over short-term wants.

Residual Income
Money that keeps coming in after the work is done—like royalties, licensing fees, or rent. Also known as passive income.

Return on Investment (ROI)
A measure of how much profit or value you gain from an investment, compared to what you put in. Usually shown as a percentage.

Savings
Money you set aside and don't spend. It's your financial safety net and a key to flexibility and freedom.

Self-Liquidating Debt
Borrowed money used to buy or build something that pays for itself—like a vending machine business or rental property that covers the loan with its income.

System
A repeatable structure that handles tasks or generates income with less effort over time. Systems are how wealth scales.

Wealth
The accumulation of valuable assets that generate income or security. True wealth creates freedom—not just more spending power

CITATIONS & FOOTNOTES

Chapter One: Money Is a Mirror

1. Klontz, Brad, et al. *Mind Over Money: Overcoming the Money Disorders That Threaten Our Financial Health*. Broadway Books, 2009.

2. Furnham, Adrian, and Barrie Gunter. *Money Madness: The Psychology of Saving, Spending, Loving, and Hating Money*. Routledge, 1991.

3. Piff, Paul K., et al. "Higher Social Class Predicts Increased Unethical Behavior." *Proceedings of the National Academy of Sciences*, vol. 109, no. 11, 2012, pp. 4086–4091.

4. Ariely, Dan. *Predictably Irrational: The Hidden Forces That Shape Our Decisions*. Harper Perennial, 2009.

5. Lerner, Jennifer S., et al. "Emotion and Decision Making." *Annual Review of Psychology*, vol. 66, 2015, pp. 799–823.

6. O'Neill, Barbara. "Managing Sudden Money." *Rutgers Cooperative Extension*, 2016.

7. Kahneman, Daniel. *Thinking, Fast and Slow*. Farrar, Straus and Giroux, 2011.

8. Duhigg, Charles. *The Power of Habit: Why We Do What We Do in Life and Business*. Random House, 2012.

Chapter Two: Develop Your Relationship With Money

1. Klontz, Brad, and Ted Klontz. *Mind Over Money: Overcoming the Money Disorders That Threaten Our Financial Health*. Broadway Books, 2009.

2. Furnham, Adrian, and Barrie Gunter. *Money Madness: The Psychology of Saving, Spending, Loving, and Hating Money*. Routledge, 1991.

3. Piff, Paul K., et al. "Having Less, Giving More: The Influence of Social Class on Prosocial Behavior." *Journal of Personality and Social Psychology*, vol. 99, no. 5, 2010, pp. 771–784.

4. Taylor, Keeanga-Yamahtta. *Race for Profit: How Banks and the Real Estate Industry Undermined Black Homeownership*. University of North Carolina Press, 2019.

5. Gurney, Tamara. "Your Financial Script: The Subconscious Pattern Running Your Money Life." *Forbes*, 15 Mar. 2023.

6. Ariely, Dan. *Predictably Irrational: The Hidden Forces That Shape Our Decisions*. Harper Perennial, 2009.

7. Kahneman, Daniel. *Thinking, Fast and Slow*. Farrar, Straus and Giroux, 2011.

8. Dunn, Elizabeth, and Michael Norton. *Happy Money: The Science of Happier Spending*. Simon & Schuster, 2013.

9. Duhigg, Charles. *The Power of Habit: Why We Do What We Do in Life and Business*. Random House, 2012.

Chapter Three: Habits Beat Zeroes

1. Klontz, Brad, and Ted Klontz. *Mind Over Money: Overcoming the Money Disorders That Threaten Our Financial Health*. Broadway Books, 2009.

2. Ariely, Dan. *Predictably Irrational: The Hidden Forces That Shape Our Decisions*. Harper Perennial, 2009.

3. Kahneman, Daniel. *Thinking, Fast and Slow*. Farrar, Straus and Giroux, 2011.

4. Clear, James. *Atomic Habits: An Easy & Proven Way to Build Good Habits & Break Bad Ones*. Avery, 2018.

5. Ramsey, Dave. *The Total Money Makeover: A Proven Plan for Financial Fitness*. Thomas Nelson, 2003.

6. Mullainathan, Sendhil, and Eldar Shafir. *Scarcity: Why Having Too Little Means So Much*. Times Books, 2013.

7. Duhigg, Charles. *The Power of Habit: Why We Do What We Do in Life and Business*. Random House, 2012.

8. Furnham, Adrian, and Barrie Gunter. *Money Madness: The Psychology of Saving, Spending, Loving, and Hating Money*. Routledge, 1991

Chapter Four: When More Money Makes Things Worse

1. Klontz, Brad, and Ted Klontz. *Mind Over Money*. Broadway Books, 2009.

2. Kahneman, Daniel. *Thinking, Fast and Slow*. Farrar, Straus and Giroux, 2011.

3. Shapiro, Thomas M. *The Hidden Cost of Being African American: How Wealth Perpetuates Inequality*. Oxford University Press, 2004.

4. Ariely, Dan. *The Upside of Irrationality: The Unexpected Benefits of Defying Logic at Work and at Home*. Harper Perennial, 2011.

5. Collins, Chuck, and Jennifer Ladd. *Assets and the Poor: A New American Welfare Policy*. Brookings Institution Press, 1991.

6. Stanley, Thomas J., and William D. Danko. *The Millionaire Next Door: The Surprising Secrets of America's Wealthy*. Taylor Trade Publishing, 1996.

7. Duhigg, Charles. *The Power of Habit*. Random House, 2012.

8. La'More, Robyn. *The Colors of Money™*. Internal system cited in Chapter 19.

Chapter Five: The Myth of "High Income"

1. Warren, Elizabeth, and Amelia Warren Tyagi. *The Two-Income Trap: Why Middle-Class Parents Are Going Broke*. Basic Books, 2003.

2. Frank, Robert H. *Luxury Fever: Why Money Fails to Satisfy in an Era of Excess*. Princeton University Press, 1999.

3. Matousek, Mark. "36% of Americans Earning $250,000 or More Say They Live Paycheck to Paycheck." *CNBC*, 30 Aug. 2022, www.cnbc.com.

Chapter Six: A High Earner Going Nowhere?

1. Pew Research Center. "What Is the Middle Class? Income and Trends." *Pew Research*, 2022, www.pewresearch.org.

2. Acemoglu, Daron, and Pascual Restrepo. "Robots and Jobs: Evidence from US Labor Markets." *Journal of Political Economy*, vol. 128, no. 6, 2020, pp. 2188–2244.

3. Kiyosaki, Robert T. *Rich Dad's Guide to Investing: What the Rich Invest in That the Poor and Middle Class Do Not!*. Plata Publishing, 2000.

Chapter Seven: Control vs. Growth

1. Fisher, Kenneth L., and Lara W. Hoffmans. *The Ten Roads to Riches: The Ways the Wealthy Got There (And How You Can Too!)* Wiley, 2008.
2. Bogle, John C. *The Little Book of Common Sense Investing: The Only Way to Guarantee Your Fair Share of Stock Market Returns.* Wiley, 2007.
3. Klontz, Brad, and Ted Klontz. *Mind Over Money.* Broadway Books, 2009.

Chapter Eight: Sacrifice Is Sacred
Angelou, Maya. "You'll never be great at anything for which you are not willing to sacrifice." Quoted in interview, widely attributed. Source appears in multiple public addresses and conversations; no definitive original publication located.

Chapter Nine: This Isn't a 401(k) Book...
No citations required. Financial perspectives presented reflect the author's framework for accelerated wealth-building and do not constitute individualized financial advice.

Chapter Ten: First, the Parachute
No citations required. Financial perspectives presented reflect the author's framework for accelerated wealth-building and do not constitute individualized financial advice.

Chapter Eleven: When You Shouldn't Invest (Yet)
1. Buffett, Warren. *Berkshire Hathaway Annual Shareholder Letters.* Berkshire Hathaway, 1977–present.
2. "Investing." *Investopedia*, Dotdash Meredith, www.investopedia.com/investing-4427785. Accessed 14 July 2025.

Chapter Twelve: Spending at a Discount Is Not Saving
No citations required. Financial perspectives presented reflect the author's framework for accelerated wealth-building and do not constitute individualized financial advice.

Chapter Thirteen: The Psychology of Liquidity
There are no external citations required for this chapter. All material is original insight, common financial principles, or author-created frameworks (such as the Liquidity Shield). The "Green Money" reference and *Colors of Money™*system are proprietary to Color Of Money LLC and do not require citation beyond internal consistency.

Chapter Fourteen: Pay Yourself First Isn't Just a Saying
Benartzi, Shlomo, and Richard H. Thaler. "Save More Tomorrow™: Using Behavioral Economics to Increase Employee Saving." *Journal of Political Economy*, vol. 112, no. S1, 2004, pp. S164–S187.

Chapter Fifteen: Money Math for Real Life
No citations required. Financial perspectives presented reflect the author's framework for accelerated wealth-building and do not constitute individualized financial advice.

Chapter Sixteen: Uncle Sam, Your Silent Partner
1. Social Security Administration. "Contribution and Benefit Base." *SSA.gov*, 2025, www.ssa.gov/OACT/COLA/cbb.html. Accessed 14 July 2025.

Chapter Seventeen: The Asset Advantage

1. Internal Revenue Service. "Topic No. 409 Capital Gains and Losses." *IRS.gov*, www.irs. gov/taxtopics/tc409. Accessed 14 July 2025.

Chapter Eighteen: The Game Is Rigged—So Learn to Play

No citations required. Financial perspectives presented reflect the author's framework for accelerated wealth-building and do not constitute individualized financial advice.

Chapter Nineteen: The Colors of Money

There are no external citations required for this chapter. All material is original insight, common financial principles, or author-created frameworks (such as *The Colors of Money™*). The *Colors of Money™* frameworks are proprietary to Color Of Money LLC and do not require citation beyond internal consistency.

Chapter Twenty: Seeds vs. Fruit

There are no external citations required for this chapter. All material is original insight, common financial principles, or author-created frameworks (such as *The Colors of Money™*). The *Colors of Money™* frameworks are proprietary to Color Of Money LLC and do not require citation beyond internal consistency.

Chapter Twenty-One: Money by the Move vs. Money by the Month

There are no external citations required for this chapter. All material is original insight, common financial principles, or author-created frameworks (such as *The Colors of Money™*). *The Colors of Money™* frameworks are proprietary to Color Of Money LLC and do not require citation beyond internal consistency.

Chapter Twenty-Two: Systems Beat Hustle

No citations required. Financial perspectives presented reflect the author's framework for accelerated wealth-building and do not constitute individualized financial advice.

Chapter Twenty-Three: What a System Looks Like

No citations required. Financial perspectives presented reflect the author's framework for accelerated wealth-building and do not constitute individualized financial advice.

Chapter Twenty-Four: How to Build Your Own System

No citations required. Financial perspectives presented reflect the author's framework for accelerated wealth-building and do not constitute individualized financial advice.

Chapter Twenty-Five: No System, No Scale

Gerber, Michael E. *The E-Myth Revisited: Why Most Small Businesses Don't Work and What to Do About It.* HarperBusiness, 1995.

Chapter Twenty-Six: Passive Isn't Perfect

Internal system citation: The Colors of Money™. All concepts relating to passive income lanes, system stages, and income behavior are derived from the author's proprietary financial framework.

Chapter Twenty-Seven: The Difference Between a Job, a Gig, a Hustle, & a Business
This chapter contains original frameworks and definitions based on the author's internal system, including *The Colors of Money™*.
No external citations are required.

Chapter Twenty-Eight: Learn to Negotiate Oranges
This chapter contains original storytelling and negotiation frameworks developed by the author.
No external citations are required.

Chapter Twenty-Nine: The Success Team Roster
No external citation needed (*original content*).
Includes internal system reference: *The Colors of Money™*.

Chapter Thirty: Change Your Life
No external citation needed. This chapter is 100% original content, including the "Orange Fund Rule" and all related frameworks.
Includes internal system reference: *The Colors of Money™*

Chapter Thirty-One: Small Bucks, Big Gains
No external citation needed. All strategies, analogies, and flip examples are original or based on widely known, common-market practices (e.g., reselling used goods, offering freelance services). No copyrighted content, proprietary terms, or quotations are used.
[1] *Internal system created by the author: The Colors of Money™.*

Chapter Thirty-Two: The Flip List
No external citation needed. All flipping strategies, platforms, and market ideas are drawn from original analysis or public knowledge sources (e.g., resale platforms like eBay, OfferUp, Mercari). No proprietary frameworks or quoted content was used.
[1] *Internal system created by the author: The Colors of Money™.*

Chapter Thirty-Three: Flip Up or Flip Down
No external citation needed. All strategies, metaphors, and capital allocation concepts are original to the author. The ideas align with broader financial education principles but are not derived from or quoting any specific published material. This chapter includes references to the The Colors of Money™ system, particularly Orange Money (capital gains).
[1] *Internal system created by the author: The Colors of Money™.*

Chapter Thirty-Four: Leverage vs. Lifestyle
No external citation needed. All analysis, warnings about credit systems, and comparisons between lifestyle debt vs. capital leverage are original to the author, reflecting personal financial philosophy and strategic frameworks. This chapter makes direct use of the The Colors of Money™ system and defines Red Money (consumer credit) and White Money (savings).
[1] *Internal system created by the author: The Colors of Money™.*

Chapter Thirty-Five: When Refinance Makes Dollars and Cents

No external citation needed. This chapter is built entirely from original author insights and strategic frameworks regarding leverage, risk mitigation, and responsible refinance behavior. This chapter uses and expands on internal concepts from the The Colors of Money™ system. Specifically:

Bronze Money = strategic, self-liquidating business credit

Red Money = consumer or personally-serviced debt

[1] *Internal system created by the author: The Colors of Money™*

Chapter Thirty-Six: Escape Velocity🚀

No external citation needed. This chapter is entirely original in its metaphorical use of "escape velocity" as a framework for describing financial independence. While the term "escape velocity" originates in physics, its use here is conceptual and does not require a citation under MLA guidelines. This chapter implicitly builds on concepts from earlier chapters including The Colors of Money™, particularly the transition away from labor-based income (Blue Money) and the strategic use of Orange, Yellow, and Green Money.

[1] *Internal system created by the author: The Colors of Money™.*

Chapter Thirty-Seven: Opportunity Knocks Again (and Again)

The phrase "Opportunity knocks" is a well-known idiom in the public domain, and the reinterpretation presented here is original. The chapter builds conceptually from earlier content within the book. This chapter contains a direct reference to The Colors of Money™, which is the author's proprietary framework.

[1] *Internal system created by the author: The Colors of Money™.*

Chapter Thirty-Eight: The Fast Lane Isn't the Scam—It's the Strategy

No external sources cited. All examples and frameworks are original to the author.

[1] *Internal system created by the author: The Colors of Money™.*

Chapter Thirty-Nine: Teaching Will Help You Learn

No external sources cited. All examples and frameworks are original to the author.

[1] *Internal system created by the author: The Colors of Money™.*

Chapter Forty: Where From Here?

Internal system citation: The Colors of Money™. Developed by the author, Robyn La'More. All framework references are original and expanded in Chapter Nineteen and the forthcoming companion book. Financial perspectives presented reflect the author's framework for accelerated wealth-building and do not constitute individualized financial advice.

[1] *Internal system created by the author: The Colors of Money™*

A WORD FROM THE AUTHOR

A Personal Note from the Author

Sharing these concepts, ideas, and principles about money has been a tremendous honor. This book is me acting on my own advice.

Although I've studied money for years and experienced real success, I often defaulted to undisciplined habits. I moved with inertia instead of intention.

Over the years, I made financial sacrifices I knew I shouldn't have made—often out of duty and honor. So when betrayal hit, I was shell-shocked. And financially fragile. Then my father—my hero—died. Beyond the heartbreak, I was left with expenses and income gaps that nearly broke me.

I needed every color of money imaginable—and I needed it all at once.

I worked for Blue Money fifteen hours a day. I devoted 90% of my off-hours—and 40% of that Blue Money—to building a Teal Money venture. I committed myself to monetizing one of my deepest passions: writing.

Television and film production have always been my first loves—powerful storytelling tools, paths my heart still leads me toward. But they're expensive to launch. Writing became the most accessible path forward.

So I charged forth into fiction.

During the hardest year of my life, I wrote *Pyrrhic Victoria*, my first psychological drama novel with a strong erotic edge. Since then, I've written three more novels in the series, all ready to launch over the next year. I'm currently outlining the fifth and final installment while developing several standalone novels simultaneously.

My publishing company, Sticky Novels, specializes in psychological thrillers for adults—available in both censored and uncensored editions. You're welcome to explore my work at **StickyNovels.com**.

I also felt the need to share hard-earned lessons and years of research. For a long time, I thought I had to cross the finish line of a personal net worth in the tens of millions before I could teach anyone else. But I realized that was a trap—and a delay tactic. People who need and want what I have to offer will use it. They'll incorporate the lessons and research for their own benefit, without wasting time trying to discredit me.

And those who are prone to that behavior? They're swinging a double-edged sword.

If you have a net worth of a hundred million, they'll say, "Sure, that works for you—but you can't relate to me."

If you're still on the path—still building—they'll say, "You're not even there yet—what do you know?"

That's when I decided to stop waiting. I launched Colors of Money LLC, not just to teach what school didn't—but to build a legacy of financial freedom for people like me.

This book—*School Didn't Teach You That*—is just the first move. If it sparked action in you, thank you. Your investment supports your own financial path—and helps fund mine.

When you begin to make progress, tell someone. Tell me. Tell the next person. There are many ways out of financial struggle—but every path forward requires focus.

Wishing you clarity, courage, and a future of Green Money.

See you in the next book.

— *The Author*
Ms. Robyn La'More

STAY CONNECTED

WITH

COLORS OF MONEY LLC

The conversation doesn't stop here.

If *School Didn't Teach You That* inspired you, challenged your thinking, or gave you tools you're excited to use—stay in the loop. The journey to financial freedom is not a one-and-done event. It's a movement.

Here's how you can stay connected:

- 📬 **Join the Newsletter**

Get exclusive insights, tools, and first-look announcements about the upcoming companion book *The Colors of Money™*, plus access to new tools, courses, and live sessions.

- 🎯 **Be the First to Know**

Get early updates on **The Colors of Money™ Board Game**, investment toolkits, and the full curriculum series.

- 🧠 **Share Your Wins**

Tell us how the book helped you. Inspire someone else. Your breakthrough might spark someone else's.

Subscribe now at:
👉 TheColorsOfMoney.com

You can also follow on social media @ColorsOfMoney or @StickyNovels depending on the journey you're on.

The next chapter of your financial freedom story starts now

Post Script: *Robyn La'More also writes psychological thrillers for adult readers under her pen name* **Jade Green**.

Explore her fiction work at **StickyNovels.com**.

COMING SOON

The Colors of Money™: The Book

You've seen the system.

Now learn how to **build your financial life around it**.

Deep-dive into the full framework that's quietly helped hundreds of high-achievers rethink money—not just how to earn it, but how to move it, multiply it, and manage it like a pro.

This isn't theory. It's strategy.

The Colors of Money™: The Book
Arriving Soon
Join the waitlist at TheColorsOfMoney.com

Post Script: *Robyn La'More also writes psychological thrillers for adult readers under her pen name* **Jade Green**.
Explore her fiction work at **StickyNovels.com**.